ADAM S. FALKENSTEINER

Alcohol

addicted or not addicted,
that is the question!

AF208633

There is only one way.

Alcohol

addicted or not addicted, that is the question!

When, at the end of the book, you say with full conviction:

"Alcohol? I'm not stupid!"

Then you will have regained control of your life and my work will be done.

Herstellung und Verlag: BoD – Books on Demand,
Norderstedt
ISBN: 9783756890224

FOREWORD

There were times when I liked to drink. Parties, exuberance, happiness, fun and sex. Then there were times of anxiety, inadequacy and depression. I hated drinking and thought I was too weak to give it up. So I kept drinking, stumbling from one excess to the next, while the periods of sobriety became more and more remorseful and painful.

The hours I missed at work piled up. I was often sick and unable to do regular work. Yet I was able to keep my addiction a secret. What a feat.

The real problem with alcoholism, as I see it, is this:

The addictive substance is freely available, and more importantly, almost everywhere. It is relatively cheap, and almost everyone uses it. And with this amount of consumers, the individual is really lost. So it is hard to tell who has an addiction problem and who does not.

Of course I know that not everyone who drinks alcohol is a "drinker". I also have no interest in labeling everyone an alcoholic just because I have an addiction problem and don't want to be alone with it.

My desire is to show people that they are not alone and that addiction can even bring them many positive insights that they could never experience without the alcohol problem. The person who is in the middle of it may not be able to understand at the moment that there are some positive aspects hidden in the addiction, but it is exactly this realization that is the way out in the end.

One thing I am sure of is that the line between "normal" drinking and "addictive" drinking is not always clear. That is the great danger: we do not feel when we cross the invisible line. That's why the examples in this book show the first signs of "addictive drinking," which sooner or later ends in addiction.

Group discussions, therapies and personal experiences with addiction give a realistic background to the content.

Alcohol abuse is a very serious subject, but I also want to show the reader that abstinence can have many positive aspects, once you have changed your attitude. People who live with an alcoholic and do not have a problem with alcohol themselves will also get suggestions on how they can behave better in the future, in order to be helpful to their addicted partner and, above all, to be able to cope with their partner's addiction more easily.

Alcoholism is a widespread disease and yet relatively unexplored from a medical point of view. My book is not a theoretical or scientific treatise, but a practical guide that describes the disease from the perspective of "ex-alcoholics" (Note: I have used the term "EX-alcoholic" only for the sake of simplicity. Actually, it should not be used, because ex-alcoholics do not exist in the strict sense of the word. Once an alcoholic - always an alcoholic. One merely changes one's state; one is either "wet" or "dry. Further definitions will follow elsewhere) will be explained in more detail and ways out will be shown to those affected. First and foremost, I want to give you the opportunity to make peace. Make peace with what was, with your family, with society, and last but not least, make peace with your deepest inner self, your soul.

There is definitely no pill that cures addiction, even though the pharmaceutical industry has often published euphoric success stories in the past. Alcoholism is a disease that can be treated and recognized as such, but it cannot be cured.

This is probably why we are so afraid of it and its consequences. And it is this fear that I want to take away. Alcoholism is indeed incurable, but you can stop it at any time.

Even though it is officially a disease, I prefer not to call it a disease. Anyone who has stopped drinking and has been sober for a long time will tell you that you don't feel sick at all once you start on the road to sobriety. On the contrary, undreamt-of powers and previously "drowned" sensations return, making life worth living again. Disease only slumbers within us as long as we do not give it permission to become active again. It is only a question of whether we give it power over us or not.

So one thing is very clear: "Without a firm will, it does not work. But will alone is not enough.

A strong will usually comes from a strong ego. And unfortunately, the ego is often the reason for every failure, in every situation in life. Actions initiated by the ego usually end in disaster. Therefore, it is imperative that you first get to the bottom of your ego before you can successfully overcome your alcohol problem.

And to understand how the ego works, you must first acknowledge that you have one, and then recognize when it is currently influencing your actions and thoughts. Only when we know that the ego is the source of our beliefs can we take countermeasures. That is why I devote an entire chapter at the end of the book to this topic. Take the time to understand yourself and your inner processes and patterns, for with your deep understanding of your uniqueness you will solve all problems with ease.

But first, learn what's behind alcoholism, what causes it, and what are the ways out. Make this formula your tool:

Awareness + Will + Knowledge = Freedom

If you want to live a happy life, it will be helpful for you to learn that taking back the power over your own life is inevitable.
However, you will only succeed in this conquest if you stop blaming other people, situations, experiences, and circumstances for your perceived failures. For first of all, there is no such thing as guilt, only responsibility, and consequently there is no such thing as failure, only results.
And results are the result of intentions, whether conscious or unconscious. Only our judgments, whether negative or positive, make a result a failure or a success.

The fatal thing about giving away guilt is that I also give away my power. Guilt and power are so intertwined that we do not perceive them as two separate things. We believe that if someone else is to blame for something, we are innocent. The true conclusion, however, is that when we give away the blame, we also give away the responsibility and the power. Because to whom I give the blame, I also give the power.

Please think about this.

So if someone else has the power, you are powerless at his mercy. You have no control over your own destiny. People who blame others for their failures are like rebellious children: "It's not my fault, he started it," or "If you weren't so bad-tempered all the time, I wouldn't have to go to the pub.
If you want to take control of your problems, you must learn to take full responsibility for your life. No one but yourself can

change anything in your life.

Consider the following testimonials and insights as useful tools that will put the power of your will on the right track right from the start on the road to a happy, "sober" future.

Nothing is more important than your personal well-being. Only when you are able to enjoy a life without alcohol will you stay sober and healthy. As long as you mourn the "good times," you will keep your old patterns alive.

Since we naturally struggle with the "long, rocky road," don't think of your efforts as a sacrifice that your family and society are asking you to make in order to make your life miserable, but rather as a unique opportunity to give your life a new, positive meaning.

Of course, in order to truly learn from the experiences you have described, you must be completely honest. By honesty, I mean your sober recognition that you have a problem with alcohol. Only you can decide if it is time to accept help.

First of all, this book offers you the opportunity to open up to your problem on your own. If you do not find all the answers to your questions in this book, you should seek out experienced people with whom you can work together on a long-term basis.

Even a skydiver can't just strap on a parachute and jump out of a plane. He must first take courses that teach him the necessary basic skills so that his first jump is not his last.

As you can imagine, a basic course and a jump are not enough to survive future jumps. This requires constant practice.

Consider reading this as your own personal basic course, and then get the other practical "training" by attending a regular group, such as Alcoholics Anonymous, Blue Cross, etc.

I can promise you one thing right now. You will be surprised at how many "normal" people you will meet.

You will always be understood and taken seriously. Because these people have gone through the same thing that is happening to you or may happen to you. Soon you will find out that you are not alone with your problems and that there are thousands of possible solutions.

Even if you feel queasy at first about exposing yourself to other people, don't lose sight of your goal and jump over your shadow.

There may not be many opportunities to do so.

Think of the happy years ahead of you and never forget what alcohol has done to you in the past and what the consequences of "continuing to drink" would be for you. Don't be discouraged by statistics that say only a small percentage of addicts make it to sobriety.

From my own group experience, I can assure you that almost all of the people I met in the group at the beginning of my dry season are still enjoying it. So I can contradict all the official statistics:

"95% of energetic addicts remain permanently sober".

This very positive result helps much more than any impersonal, factual statistic.

By the way, a lofty goal is easier to achieve if you focus on each step. Each small step takes us further, even if it seems tiny and insignificant compared to the distance ahead.

Almost without exception, mountaineers talk about the exertion that each climb brings. They also say that they do not constantly stare at the summit during the ascent, because the constant awareness of the distance still to be covered is more paralyzing than stimulating, because a great goal inspires great awe on closer inspection. It shows one more than clearly how small one is at the moment. That is why the climber concentrates on every single step. Of course, the goal is indispensable, for why else would he take the many small steps if he did not know where they would lead him? So the goal serves as a target. It gives a clear direction. The individual steps each represent their own small stage goal, which has a less awe-inspiring effect on us and is therefore grasped by our mind as easy to achieve. A small step is easy. Anyone can do it. But it is in the sum of these small steps that the success, the great goal, which before seemed almost unattainable, is achieved.

In this way, the mountaineer climbs the mountain step by step until he can finally enjoy the overwhelming view.

For an alcoholic, every day he doesn't drink is a success. In sports, success is rewarded with medals. So let yourself receive a medal every day. It's up to you to decide what that medal should look like, just be careful not to get into another addiction. If you always reward your achievements with a bar of chocolate, you can expect even worse problems.

For example, a good recognition is an open look in the mirror. Look deeply into your eyes and maintain eye contact. Be proud of your accomplishment. Observe the returning clarity of your eyes and mind. Look forward to regaining your confidence and drive.

Always remember the mountaineer: "A clearly defined goal is important. But it is more important to take the first, decisive step. And to repeat that step every day with determination. Sincerely.

Adam S. Falkensteiner

INTRODUCTION

Officially, there are about 1.8 million alcoholics living in Germany. This is an impressive number. Of course, the number of unreported cases is many times higher. But one thing surprises me: If we had 1.8 million AIDS cases every year, wouldn't the entire population be on high alert? But with the high number of alcoholics, the public seems to be completely unconcerned. Why do you think that is?
If you walk through the world with your eyes open, you quickly realize that the course for addiction is set in the schoolyard.

No wonder when you look at the role models of our young people. All of us, and I am no exception, are too careless with the "drug" alcohol. In every Hollywood movie, the heroes drink to wash down their frustrations or to celebrate their successes.
Alcoholism does not stop at any social class. Drinking takes place in almost every household. Rich or poor. While the type and quality of alcoholic beverages may differ, the consequences remain the same. Even the reasons why people reach for the bottle are often similar.

In a high-tech, fast-paced time like ours, we often feel overwhelmed. Doctors' and therapists' offices are overflowing with patients suffering from neurological overload. Burnout is the most common diagnosis of the computer age.
Indeed, the flood of information to be processed continues to grow. Overstimulation, existential anxiety, and the fear of being ill-equipped for the times to come due to a lack of

education are affecting people. The times when several generations could benefit from building up their parents' business are over. Many small businesses are forced to close their doors due to fierce competition. Nothing seems to last. Before our very eyes, we are witnessing the disintegration of old, cherished values.

Change is the new consistency, get used to it. Not to do so would be fatal.

When development was even slower, people had more time to adapt to the coming changes.
Today, when you return from a two-week vacation, you may not find your desk. Instead, there will be a computer with a silicon chip brain that is far more powerful than the entire workforce. Throw in some political unrest, and the world may seem completely out of whack. Who is going to help us, and where will the help come from?
Unfortunately, more and more often from the pharmaceutical industry in the form of tranquilizers and mostly from breweries, disguised as a healthy specialty from the heart of nature.
Such promising advertising slogans are balm for our tortured souls. How much we long for the purity of nature and our original desire to belong in the face of all the pollution.

The longing for these supposedly "natural products" is now so great in Germany that we far exceed all neighboring countries in alcohol consumption. Allow me to use a casual expression, but we "drink up" Lake Constance every year.
But this kind of competition should not fill us with pride, but rather make us think. Something seems to be vehemently wrong. The fact that beer is still considered a food by the

majority of the population shows how little we know about the dangers of this national drink. Of course, beer is just a placeholder, it does not matter what we drink - beer, wine, champagne or spirits - the consequences remain the same. We are much more careful when it comes to drugs on the market, such as cocaine and heroin.

If you feel bad, you'd rather have a glass of champagne than a needle, and you don't feel guilty about it.

Those who take this stuff are more likely to be considered addicts than those who wash down their daily frustrations with a well-kept pilsner in a cozy atmosphere.

Our consciousness does not easily cope with these hard drugs. They are unknown to us. And "what the farmer doesn't know..." well, you know. This should not cause you to gain experience in this area. We don't want to focus on the so called "hard drugs", but we want to focus on "good old alcohol" and the damage it does. Of course, we don't want to admit the dangers, so we like to trivialize our consumption: "A little beer, a little wine, a little liquor". We also drink alcohol because we think it's part of life. A glass of wine with a good meal, a bottle of champagne on New Year's Eve, just like a Christmas tree is part of Christmas. For a healthy person, this is not a problem. For addicts, however, it can be a deadly trap. Our society has very clear ideas and demands. That's why we drink to be socially acceptable. But when we hit rock bottom, society wants nothing to do with us. Irony of fate. How many diseases are caused by excessive alcohol consumption, and in how many cases is alcohol consumption itself the disease?

I wrote this book for all those who are tired of suppressing the everyday worries and lies about alcohol. Drinking as such is only repression and offers no solution. It may seem that alcohol relieves suffering for the moment, but it causes much greater suffering in the long run. You will realize that the thoughtless handling of this wolf in sheep's clothing will paralyze our zest for life more than it will inspire it; in stark contrast to many advertising slogans.

Consumers are led to believe that a good sip is part of good manners.

We all just have to come back to our senses. Every low has an end, and getting over a low requires a clear mind.
Lulled into a high-proof cloud of alcohol, it's all too easy to fall into a negative vortex. "Alcohol makes your head hollow. Just listen to the conversations at a bar. With a constantly decreasing brain capacity, caused by a greatly increased alcohol level, only verbal garbage is slurred.
It would also be too easy to find the solution to one's problems in alcohol intoxication. As I said before, I do not want to lump all people who drink alcohol together. That would be an easy way, but not the right way, to deal with the problem of "alcoholism. The problem is much deeper than one might think at first glance.
I do not think about legal prohibition either. My focus is only on those who, like me, are "addicted" and look to alcohol for help.
I use the term "addicted" because alcoholism is one of many addictions. Addiction, as such, refers to the myriad of different "means" we use to "satisfy" that particular addiction. An addict has an exaggerated (pathological) need to consume things, whether cake in the case of the "food addict," nicotine in the case of the smoker, or alcohol in the case of the alcoholic, in such quantities until a desired state is achieved. Another way of saying this is "until it 'clicks' in

the brain. The addict loses touch with all "normal" problem solvers and his environment. Once the disease has broken out, walks in the woods and yoga exercises will no longer help to calm him down. The only thing that will help him is the addictive substance he has chosen.

Since alcohol is accepted by all classes as a modern drink and is therefore the most inconspicuous means of satisfying his addiction, the alcoholic finds himself in a veritable paradise in our society.

At every kiosk, in every pub, in the finest hotels, in every supermarket, even at the gas station, he has a huge choice. And he will never be prosecuted for the illegal possession of drugs.

In this way, he remains completely unrecognized for a long time. No one notices his illness as long as he doesn't go on a rampage or drink himself into a stupor.

OUR IMAGE OF THE "REAL" ALCOHOLIC

Haven't you had the same experience of strolling through the pedestrian zone of a city and encountering a horde of noisy, unkempt individuals?

Misfits, lost personalities, bums! They are loud, drink in public without restraint, have terrible manners, riot, stink and vomit wherever they walk and stand. They are conspicuous, ubiquitous in big cities, and no one can pass by without noticing them. This is exactly the image of the alcoholic that we have formed in our minds, this stinking scum!

And this image of the drinker is precisely why we find it so difficult to acknowledge our own drinking problem, let alone admit that we have one.

Who wants to put themselves on the same level as these people? "I'll never be like that," we say to ourselves and turn away, not realizing that upon closer inspection, the solution to our problem may lie there.

Precisely because no one wants to be on the same level as these people, this forms the basis of our alcohol behavior patterns and makes it difficult for us to get out.
After all, where in the world could I get out if I'm nowhere?
Too philosophical, you think? Well, let me be a little clearer. These "bums" are only a very small, insignificant part in the great swamp of alcoholism. They are just the visible outgrowth of the whole.

The majority of addicts sit unnoticed in offices, law firms, wearing uniforms and working in operating rooms, drinking in secret, at least not crying in public.

The status of the bum is that of the boogeyman. He represents all those who are too cowardly to face their addiction. They can point at him and say, "Look, he's a drunk. You can't compare me to him.
For the moment, that may be true. As long as we have a good job and a steady income, a warm, cozy apartment, we really can't compare ourselves to those people sleeping outdoors.
We lull ourselves into a sense of security, and who wants to break out of this ideal world, let alone consider such a fate possible for themselves? But if our boss has just fired us, the bank has closed our overdrawn account, the landlord has threatened to evict us if we are late with the rent again, we will not be so quick to condemn these people.
Maybe we even show a little compassion, because we

ourselves have just washed down our sorrows with a bottle of wine, and at that moment we realize that the step to a life on the street is not as big as we thought before in our illusory security.

Admittedly, this does not have too much to do with the subject of alcohol and its accompanying symptoms.

But such thoughts play an important role when we analyze our personal alcohol consumption. The way we look at our drinking behavior and the resulting length of the period of suffering is, in fact, largely due to the example of the bums (those affected know that I do not mean this expression in a derogatory way). The more aware you are of your own drinking habits, the more likely you are to feel a certain respect for a person who lives his addiction without restraint. Because it is the "bums" who are the benchmark for alcoholism in our society. They seem to drink excessively and are brutalized both internally and externally. All characteristics that we clearly do not show (at least not yet). So no one will voluntarily call themselves an alcoholic, since such a statement would lower them to a level that seems downright degrading. But where is the limit? After how many bottles of beer does the descent begin?

In no area is there so much comparing and lying as in testing or disclosing one's alcohol consumption.

The "wet" alcoholic judges the severity of his disease solely by the "required" amount. He literally looks for people who drink even more than he does to prove to himself that his consumption is still in the "normal" range. Insanity!!!

Once you've found one, and you usually don't have to look very far, the goal of trivializing your illness, not to mention rejecting it outright, is achieved. Alcoholism is a disease, and a stomach ulcer is a disease. In fact, a stomach ulcer is often used as a figurehead when one is in a slump. A good reason to get sympathy from others: "Poor guy has too much on his plate". In most cases, however, the stomach ulcer is the result of excessive alcohol consumption, but this fact is not the focus of attention; instead, it is supposedly stress at work. Stress, in turn, is the basis for burnout. The diagnosis "burnout" itself is even a kind of medal of honor for particularly hard-working employees. The fact that they are unable to perform because of their unhealthy lifestyle, which is why they became ill in the first place, is another story that is never told. In this way, the "honorably ill" person is elevated to the role of victim, and his fellow human beings pity him.

Hardly anyone will claim "I'm an alcoholic" if he or she is no longer able to excel in business or in private life. The cliché of the alcoholic is simply too negative. No one wants to identify with him. No one feels sorry for a drunk.

You don't make him chamomile tea when he feels bad. He is alone with his disease.

At this point I would like to emphasize that I am not trying to protect the alcoholic, or even pity him unduly, but rather to wake up those who are afraid of the shame of being counted among the addicts and thus inevitably running toward the abyss.

What the hell is worse - to walk around in a fog all the time, possibly endangering your own life and the lives of innocent people in traffic, perhaps beating your wife and children while intoxicated? Or to simply admit his disease and change his life from the ground up? The alcoholic has a wonderful gift. A gift that very few receive. And that gift is the chance to rebuild his life from the ground up.

There are two sides to everything. I can spend the rest of my life feeling sorry for myself for having such a difficult fate, or I can thank God for giving me the opportunity to grow physically and spiritually in this task. As soon as the sick person truly understands his situation and sees prospects for his future, he will break the cycle and come to terms with his illness.

At the risk of repeating myself, I usually avoid using the word "disease," but this word has often helped me not to always "blame" myself for my addiction. Blame only makes things worse. Guilt is always destructive and prevents positive development.

The "disease" is an excellent crutch in the beginning to help you focus on your recovery. When one is afflicted with an illness, it is better to speak of bad luck or fate than of guilt.

But - and this is the crucial point - the illness is not a free pass to continue drinking and then say apologetically, "I had to drink again. I'm just sick.

For the dry alcoholic, it is not a conspicuous disease that makes him permanently disabled or incapable of living. No, after a period of sobriety, he will actually feel better and more capable than ever before.

As I said in the preface, nothing works without a firm will. But will alone is not enough.

To understand and accept addiction, we need information. It doesn't help to fall into self-pity with the question, "Why me? Funnily enough, when you talk to addicts, you often find that at first the very thought of permanent abstinence causes them great horror, an endless emptiness and panic. No one can really imagine a party without alcohol at the beginning of dryness. What will our colleagues at the regulars' table say if we order an apple spritzer or lemonade instead of the usual beer?

What will we say if our boss offers us a glass of champagne at a company event? What do my colleagues think when I thank them but decline?

All of these questions are waiting to be answered. Together, we will find those answers in this book. But first, take some time to familiarize yourself with the subject.

Sure, almost all health insurance companies offer pamphlets that describe the classic course of alcoholism. In my opinion, however, a report on a particular disease and its causes alone is not enough to thwart it. How often do we read that a little more exercise is good for the cardiovascular system, or about the consequences of eating fatty foods?

And yet we still use the elevator when it would be healthier to take the stairs. We also too often choose a dripping pork knuckle over a fat-free, much healthier diet.

We have to realize deep down that we have to do something for our health, finally turn that "have to" into a "like to" and finally be proud of what we are doing.

Then we are truly on the best path to physical and mental health.

Of course, educational pamphlets often provide the impetus for recognizing one's own situation. Of course I can push a car that won't start.

But if the tank is empty, you will soon come to a standstill. If you're on a hill, you'll even go backwards faster than you'd like.

So make sure you fill your tank, i.e. take in information, process it, implement it, love it, live it, so that you can enjoy the results with satisfaction.

ALCOHOL AND ITS PLACE VALUE

Alcohol plays an especially important role in the lives of alcoholics. Nothing goes without a good drink. The addict drinks before an important meeting with his boss, before and during a party, on sad and happy occasions.

If there is no reason, he will find one. In short, he plans his life around alcohol.
Alcohol is at the center of everything he does.
It is not possible for him to enjoy life to the fullest without preparing all the "drinking opportunities" in detail.

For example, if the alcoholic is invited to a family party where, as he knows from previous occasions, only coffee drinkers will be present, he administers the necessary amount to himself at home in order to get through the undesirable occasion as quietly as possible, if he shows up at all. But if he does attend, he misses out on all the socializing. In fact, he misses out on the conversation because his thoughts are secretly focused on the bottle waiting for him at home.

The addiction also prevents him from having deep conversations, and he may even be distracted by other people's problems.
He is like a puppet, and the puppeteer is called "alcohol.

Even when one is not "necessarily" addicted, alcohol takes on a serious meaning (we will address this point in chapter 2 on the messengers of addiction). A New Year's Eve celebration without the obligatory glass of champagne or high-proof punch is not a real New Year's Eve celebration for us.

Unconsciously, we shape our lives with alcohol. For most of us this is not a big danger, but for a vulnerable person it can have fatal consequences.

While the "healthy" person enjoys these occasions, the "vulnerable" person inevitably slides into ruin and ends up alone.

So the question here is, "Do we really always need a mood enhancer, or can we be fun and frolicsome without one? After all, it's a wonderful feeling to wake up the morning after a party, maybe a little tired, but without a headache and with a full memory.

All the jokes from the night before flash through your mind. Conversations with other guests are still present. Isn't that a double pleasure? Surely you wouldn't be dealing with alcohol so intensely if you weren't worried about your drinking habits. So start at this point with your personal inventory. Remember when and how much you drank, on what occasions.

Recall the feelings you experienced and replay these scenarios in your mind's eye as if you were sober.

What was really good and what was really bad? How would the evening have gone if you hadn't been drinking?

To truly become the master of your alcohol problem, it is of the utmost importance to remove alcohol from its throne.

Stop being enslaved. You are a free person who cannot be told what to do. And if you are still so often asked to celebrate the New Year with champagne, resolutely say "NO, thank you.

To really stand behind the "NO" with personal respect, you

must not make alcohol a priority. Don't look back sadly on the "good" times when you drank the night away. Upon closer inspection, those supposedly good times may not have been so good.

As humans, we have a natural tendency to remember the good things and suppress the less pleasant experiences. The brain wants to protect us from pain. That's why most people who have had a bad accident don't remember it. Listen to men who talk about their military service. Although they cursed the wasted time, today they remember only the funny events.

So, consciously begin to trace the negative experiences of your life. Make a list and you will find that alcohol usually made these moments worse.

As a next step, imagine how cheerfully and calmly you will face future difficulties without asking your "friend alcohol" for help. Soon you will be able to look in the mirror with compassion. Step by step, you will begin a new life free from addiction.

ALCOHOL AS A MEANS TO AN END
WHY DO I DRINK?

This question is very different from "Why me?
What am I getting at?
"Why me?" reflects desperation: "Poor me?" With this question you make yourself the plaything of a supernatural power. The consequences are: Helplessness, hopelessness, powerlessness.

It is absolutely impossible to find a satisfactory, purposeful answer to this question.

Well, a geneticist might tell you, "Unfortunately, you have faulty DNA. It will probably be another 150 years before we can do anything about it. Would that answer have lessened your alcohol problem? Or could you now, with that medical diagnosis, go on as before and completely destroy your life and that of your family?

I don't think so. Since you decided to buy this book, you want to change your life, learn to live with addiction, and be free.

Congratulations! You are now taking the scepter in your hand!

For even if the geneticist's statement were true, what good would it do you? Instead, ask yourself the honest question: "WHY do I drink?" or "WHY did I drink?"

Why do people drink in the first place? From a purely medical standpoint, to protect the body from dehydration. Since the body is largely composed of water, water is also the best beverage to provide the cells with the fluid they need. The actual amount of water (preferably still water) that the body needs is 11/2 to 2 liters per day. In addition to quantity, the quality of the water should also be considered.

Of course, water intake has nothing to do with drinking alcohol, which is the real reason for this book, but it is directly related to the alcohol problem. This is because most of the time an alcoholic hardly consumes pure water, at least not in the amount he needs. Every time the body signals - "I need liquid" - this natural impulse is linked to the addiction. The addict feels the need for alcohol instead of providing the body with the water it needs. Even though beer and wine are mostly water, the alcohol they contain has a negative effect on the organs by depriving the body's cells of water and drying them out.

The natural feeling of thirst is then translated as "I must drink alcohol. In this way, the addict reinforces his behavioral patterns and ensures that his body becomes more and more dehydrated. Alcohol is a poison that slowly destroys cells.

The regularity with which I put an addictive substance into my body brings the addiction. Natural cues like thirst and hunger are often the triggers. To break this pattern, in the beginning you have to force yourself to drink water when you are thirsty and to keep hunger at bay by eating something, something healthy, mind you. Otherwise, alcoholism will be joined by morbid obesity.

To get to the bottom of alcoholism, the first thing to do is to find out what you are using alcohol for. Far be it from me to refer to scientific statistics that show how much alcohol is good for your health and how much is bad for your health, because statistics are simply not helpful in influencing the fate of an individual drinker. Every addict has his or her own personal patterns that need to be identified and resolved. Comparing oneself to others does not help. Everyone has to find out for himself where his limits are and what he expects from life and what quality of life he wants.

The decisive factor in "addictive drinking" is by no means the quantity. It is a false assumption that a drinker must consume large amounts of alcohol. There are people who are addicted to a bottle of beer, which is well within the "normal" range and, according to "scientific evidence," even healthy.

When I first heard this, I had to laugh. If it had only taken me one beer to "click," it would never have occurred to me that I was addicted. But when you look at it more closely, you see the little word "needed. So it takes one bottle of beer to get the desired effect, whatever that effect may be, individually. If the addict is given this bottle every day, he will not behave in a conspicuous manner.

However, if you deprive him of this ration, he may become somewhat restless. Withdrawal can then cause failure symptoms such as trembling, sweating, and irritability.

These withdrawal symptoms vary from person to person. There are no general standards. That should be enough on this subject for now. Let's look at the reasons why we can't say "no" to alcohol. Of course, there are always different reasons why someone drinks, but there is only one particular reason why we started drinking.

Recognizing these reasons, or this one reason in particular, is of the utmost importance, because it will allow us to avoid situations in the future that caused us to reach for the bottle in the past. I will not be able to look inside you. I don't see that as my job. Therefore, I will simply describe some possibilities, which you can either apply to yourself as they are, or you can add to them to find yourself in them:

- Frustration at work (too much work, not enough bread, choleric boss, disgusting co-workers, bullying, etc.)
- Inferiority complexes (feeling inferior to others in strength, appearance, ability, etc.)
- Social anxiety (fear of embarrassing oneself in front of others, fear of the opposite sex, etc.)
- Threshold anxiety (fear of new situations. Feelings of inferiority again play a role)
- Fear of failure (whether professional or personal / for men, often fear of sexual failure).
- Existential fears (loss of job, financial problems, etc.)

- Fear of life (feeling overwhelmed/fear of not being able to keep up with technological progress)
- Fear of responsibility (children, family, social status, job responsibilities, etc.)
- Fear of illness
- Fear of death
- Fear of fear

These are all fears that almost everyone has. And yet we find it very difficult to deal with them, and the approach varies from person to person.

Most of the time we equate fear with weakness. If we show our fear, we are considered weak in our own eyes. But we don't want to be called a weakling under any circumstances. So we just flush our fears down the drain. This works well for a while. But the price we pay is high. Our own lives and the lives of those who love us are at stake.

So I just ask the question: "Who is the greater weakling? The one who admits his fear and possibly seeks help from others to solve his problems (therapist, support group, wife, partner, etc.), or the one who washes down his frustration with beer and corn after work and then plays the strong Max to his worried wife and innocent children? The next day, at the latest, the fear comes back in undiminished form, enriched with feelings of guilt, which we also get delivered for free by our drunken behavior - if we still remember it.

Regardless of whether we remember it or whether our family reminds us of it, the reasons for another crash are delivered to us immediately and free of charge.

All that is needed for another crash are our guilt feelings, which now want to be drowned again. Since we do not let our problems out, and our partner sees through us like a DIA, which we consider a further disgrace, we plunge all the more into the battle with the real ruler of our lives, alcohol.

And so it goes until the partnership or marriage breaks up.

In the group I attend weekly, I almost always hear the same statement: "In my wet phase (the time when you drink), I often wished that my partner would finally leave me. Then I could at least drink in peace without being constantly reprimanded".
Some of the people I talked to, and I was no exception, were already planning what to do with their savings. This disease can go that far.
There is no classification of origin, gender or social status.
Alcohol is the only help accepted at this stage. The executioner becomes judge and confessor in one person.
So get to work immediately and share your worries and fears, however trivial they may seem, with your closest family members. If you are too embarrassed, go to a neutral person, such as your family doctor, a therapist, or ideally, a support group. You can kill two birds with one stone:
In a group, you can get your worries and fears off your chest and realize that you are not alone.
At the same time, you will learn about the dark side of alcohol from others who have been affected by it, and you will be given many approaches to solving the problem.
By the way, you will get even more advice from me in the group.
Once you get over your fear of talking about your fear, you will become more confident every day.
This does not mean that you have solved your alcohol problem. This, and this may sound a little harsh, will be with you for the rest of your life.

This thought may increase your anxiety at the moment, but don't worry, this feeling will subside - just keep reading.

In time, you will learn to appreciate your fears and worries as milestones of personal growth.

Each time you overcome these apparent hurdles, you take a step forward as a human being. Only those who swim against the current gain strength. And from now on, you will swim against the current, because we, let's call ourselves "dry-mature alcoholics," move sober and balanced in a truly "drowning" society.

ALCOHOL, THE SOCIAL DRUG

Please don't be alarmed if I come down hard on you right away. But there is a reason for this.

The sooner you recognize yourself in the situations described, the sooner you will be ready, for your own good, to join this special circle of dry alcoholics. And why it is a special circle, you will soon feel in your own body.

Observe the drinking habits of those around you. There are a few who don't drink at all, a large number of contemporaries who don't let a jug pass them by, some who drink considerably more than you do. An infinitesimally small number of those who have had bad experiences with alcohol and therefore abstain from it today, and of course those who (can) indulge in a glass every now and then.

Which category do you belong to?

Let's take a closer look at each group. In order to solve your alcohol problem, you should take a closer (more honest) look. Not to distract from yourself and not to put others in certain boxes, but out of pure self-interest. In fact, you should carefully consider from which corner you can expect the best help.

Here are some of my personal experiences:

People who have never drunk alcohol in their lives have never been very helpful to me. They could never understand my drinking. In their eyes, I will probably always remain a strange bird who is not in control of himself and his life. From these people, who are born sober, we usually get a "bloody nose" instead of the help we need. How can they ever put themselves in your shoes? They simply lack the experience and understanding.

So let's turn our attention to the people who don't let a jug pass them by. On the one hand, I used to be one of them, so I can allow myself (self-)criticism and have forgiven myself in the meantime. On the other hand, it is precisely these promille heroes who are often involved in many relapses. In your first "dry phase" you should avoid contact with these people at all costs. In the beginning, you are too "weak" to resist their stimulating slogans. Since most of these "gullible" people have a full-blown alcohol problem themselves, but are still too "weak" to get help, let alone admit their addiction, they will not understand your situation at all. These "false friends" will do everything they can to discourage you from wanting to live an abstinent life. They will call you a coward, a weakling, and so on, just to distract you from their own weaknesses. Don't make the mistake of trying to proselytize others, I'm really speaking from experience here, you're hurting yourself. You can't force anyone to be happy. Everyone has to make that decision for themselves. Just be confident that you will be envied for your courage. For every brave person is secretly envied. And this time, YOU are the brave one. Indeed, it takes quite a bit of courage to face this new task. After all, you are "almost" standing alone. I say "almost" because you have a whole army of knowledge and personalities behind you who, just like you, once started a new, balanced and sober life without any experience or background knowledge. Use this pool of knowledge as much and as often as you can and strengthen your awareness that you are never alone. You will only be truly alone when you reach for the bottle again, when your old regulars rejoice at your failure, and when your partner finally packs his bags and moves out of your shared apartment. For now, avoid all temptations to return to the bottle, and learn about and make friends with non-alcoholic beverages.

TIP: At the beginning of your dry spell, find a soft drink that you call your favorite. It should taste good to you, be readily available (e.g., a glass of mineral water with a squeeze of lemon juice), and preferably not cause any other physical harm. In other words, avoid high-calorie drinks that may taste good but will soon cause you other health problems due to obesity. By choosing a favorite drink, you are killing several birds with one stone:

You'll quickly become accustomed to this new but thoroughly healthy taste, which will make you forget about your former favorite alcoholic beverage.

In this way, they keep their bodies hydrated while satisfying their desire or need for more drinks.
They have an immediate answer when invited to a foreign country: "What do you want to drink? I have beer, wine, champagne, cognac!" You will experience this situation even more often. The host, who likes to drink, is desperately looking for someone to drink with. But as soon as you answer the question, "What would you like to drink?" as if shot from a pistol, "A mineral water with a twist of lemon," you take the

wind out of his sails and keep the upper hand. You may not be quite as sympathetic to him after expressing your "non-alcoholic" desire, but you'll get over that, won't you? (More behavioral advice to come later).

An absolutely false measure is the person who drinks even more than you do. As mentioned before, the amount you drink does not play a role in addiction. What and how much a person can tolerate depends solely on his constitution and his "standard". With regular alcohol consumption, the tolerance limit is inevitably raised in the first few years. Then nothing works without alcohol. Later, however, the tolerance level drops because the liver's performance decreases. Then nothing works even with alcohol. Even the smallest amounts affect the person and prevent him from participating in a community. So as long as you can think clearly, you should keep asking yourself: "What is the beauty of intoxication? The morning headache? The sinking feeling in my stomach? The red eyes? The shattered self-esteem the day after? Actually, it's the exuberance, the lowered inhibitions, the sudden feeling of being in control. For this we accept even the worst hangover. Let someone tell me they would drink ten bottles of beer for fun. That is just ridiculous. Real pleasure is different. It doesn't help to think that only those who drink more than you are alcoholics and that you are therefore miles away from the problem of "alcohol addiction".

The fact is that it is in our nature not to drink alcohol. Our bodies are tough and efficient. It repairs minor damage on its own without us noticing. But it is not designed to constantly process nerve toxins. When we drink alcohol, we are poisoning our body. It then fights back and tries to get rid of

the poison. This manifests itself in

- -Headaches
- -Nausea
- -faintness
- -trembling
- -sweating
- -chills
- -numbness of the skin
- -etc.

In short, the body is using all of its energy to survive.
You have the power to decide if you want to let it go on like this, or if you want to start seriously giving up poison.

Now a few words about those who only have a glass now and then. Do you think you have anything to learn from people who enjoy a glass of wine all night long? Do you think these people understand your problem? Maybe, but maybe not! It depends on how much compassion and understanding they have for your situation. Do these pleasure drinkers see through how bad and inferior we are? I would not want to put it that clearly. But we can certainly find a glimmer of truth in it.

The feeling when we (have to) pour the fifth beer while the other person is enjoying his first glass is like a hammer blow. At that moment, we must realize that our drinking behavior is not quite "normal. Recognizing this is actually a tremendous insight to keep in mind for your future alcohol-free time, isn't it?
If you approach someone with a healthy drinking pattern for

help, they may take on your problem because they may be well-adjusted and self-confident, but they certainly do not have a problem with alcohol, but they would like to know about it.

Personally, I have turned to such people from time to time in my search for help. However, I made sure that these people were absolutely loyal and reliable. It was quite possible for me to get my grief off my chest, but again, I always felt like I was talking to a dancer about football.

They just couldn't understand my problem, let alone this crushing urge to get drunk.

Each of my interlocutors from the connoisseur camp expressed their regret and pity, but none of them could show me how to get out of the vicious circle. I didn't feel any better after these conversations, despite the momentary "problem discharge" that had taken place.

Usually such an outing ended in another bender, because it became even clearer to me that I was not normal. No one could really understand what it meant to have to drink.

Helplessness and a feeling of shame that I had exposed myself in front of a "normal" person dragged me down even further. Eventually, I reached the point where I wanted to bear my fate alone. Talking to a dry alcoholic, on the other hand, is always a blessing. You hear things you already know. There are so many "aha" moments because you find yourself in the stories you hear.

Now you have found the right person to talk to. Stay on the ball. This is where your questions are finally answered. You will learn for the first time that you are "sick" - but at the same time completely normal. It is your fault that you drink, but it is not your fault that you "need" to drink.

This is the difference between sick and healthy drinking. But the insight in this statement is even more important, namely that one is not necessarily fully responsible for one's behavior during the drinking period. Alcohol takes over during this time and changes everyone.

One person becomes funny, another tired. Someone else has an increased desire for tenderness, while someone else hits everything.

Finally, you hear that you can forgive yourself. Isn't that a great relief?

But lest we lose sight of the seriousness of the matter, let me be clear: "All forgiveness has its limits. Not forgiving yourself is another "letting go" and part of the addiction. Who knows what else can happen if you keep drinking. You can forgive yourself if you have the firm intention of living your life without alcohol from now on.

Recovering alcoholics are not inhumane. They also forgive relapse. But only if you admit it immediately and then continue to work on yourself so that this is the "last" one.

Of course, you can continue as before. You decide in which condition you want to live and eventually die, no one else. Think of any help you get from me and your future therapy group as a stepping stone that will help you get a handle on your alcohol-related problems.

The problems that caused you to start drinking must be identified and resolved within yourself.

Once you have fully grasped and utilized the function of our stepping stone, you will have to dive back into the stormy ocean of life and take a few swims yourself in order not to sink again.

Do not think that without alcohol you will have no more problems. On the contrary, at the beginning of your sobriety you will be overwhelmed with problems. There is a mountain of unfinished work that you didn't have the strength to deal with while you were drinking, whether on a business or personal level. Your partner's emotional block may prove to be a real obstacle.

Remember that he or she will not be able to forget your actions of the past few years anytime soon. Now it's your turn to show understanding and patience.

Of course, no one is going to force you to get help to solve these problems. But if you want help, you will get it. Get away from the completely idiotic attitude, "I don't need a therapist. I'm not crazy!" Or "I can do this on my own!"

You know from your own experience where repressing fears and worries leads. If your marriage has been damaged by your drinking, take your partner to marriage counseling or an AA meeting.

But to avoid getting bogged down, deal with the main problem first-your alcoholism. Once you get through the first few weeks without a drop, you will be able to think more clearly and will be ready and able to take things in hand.

ALCOHOL - THE MEANS TO AN END?

The people who have relevant experience in this area all make the same statement: "I used alcohol on purpose!" If you approach this statement with the necessary attitude, you may find some parallels to your drinking behavior.

"Addiction begins with the deliberate use of the

drug!"

Since alcohol is not covered by drug laws in our country, and is also a huge source of government revenue, we can get our hands on this "poison" whenever and wherever we want, and at a relatively low price.

It is precisely this "legality" that reduces the perception of the danger inherent in it. Take away a Bavarian's mug and he is only half a man. A Frenchman without red wine is like Spain without the sea.

Alcohol has become part of our culture. It became so because it was not present from the beginning of the human species. It is not a "real" gift of Mother Earth, but an invention of man.

Only he, with his unrestrained inventive spirit, discovered and glorified this substance with all its "beautiful" side effects.

As mentioned in the beginning, alcohol is not harmful from a medical point of view, but only in very small doses.

I recently heard a doctor on the radio tell an appropriate joke on this subject:

"When a nutritionist calls his colleague and says, 'I have two pieces of news for you. One good and one bad. The good news - alcohol is healthy. The bad news is that a thimbleful is the upper limit.

If you elevate alcohol to the status of a stimulant or food, you inevitably take away its status as a drug or medicine, right?

Quite "clever" I have heard people say: "After all, monks, i.e. God-fearing people, were the originators of this cultural asset. So what can be wrong with it?"

Like our ingenuity, our repertoire of excuses is limitless. As an alcoholic, I can only say, "You're right. There is nothing wrong with alcohol itself!

In principle, a car is not dangerous in itself. However, if I get behind the wheel without any knowledge of driving and disregard all the rules of the road, such a vehicle quickly becomes a deadly weapon.
It is fundamentally necessary to put all human achievements into perspective and to question them.

A healthy person, i.e. a non-addicted person, who considers alcohol "only" as a food, will certainly be satisfied with one glass and will therefore not suffer any harm.
We must not compare ourselves with healthy people and their "natural" drinking behavior.

As soon as we drink alcohol for any reason, we have a problem. From that moment on, we have to drink!

In general, alcohol is always a means to an end. You have to realize that. Think honestly about what you enjoyed as a child. Was it juice, milk, water, or soda?
Do you remember the first time you drank from an adult's beer? I remember shaking with disgust.
We've been brainwashed since adolescence. In every movie we see heroic men washing down their frustrations with whiskey, and then we imitate them. Until we stop noticing that we are not these men and that our problems do not disappear by drinking alcohol.
We now see drinking as so normal and nothing more that it sinks us. It is only up to us whether and to what extent we allow ourselves to be enslaved by this substance.
The place value is the evil of it all. Only when you accept that

you simply cannot tolerate alcohol, and then stop punishing yourself for using it, do you take it down from its pedestal. At this point, it's best to make a list of the pros and cons of continuing to drink.

This will be very enlightening. You will be thrilled to find that accepting your disease and making the necessary changes to stop it will produce consistently satisfying results.

The following is an example of what such a list might look like:

What are the negative consequences of continuing to drink for my future life?

- Physical damage
- Psychological damage
- Loss of job
- My partner leaving me
- Financial hardship
- Social descent
- etc.

Continue the list as you wish.

What does permanent abstinence do to my personality?

- Good health
- Balance
- Vitality
- Courage to live
- An intact family life

- Self-confidence
- Etc.

Continue the list as you wish.

Such a balance will make it easier for you to decide which path is the right one. Writing down the real problems that are caused by your drinking will help you to get an overview and to stimulate yourself in a positive way.

As mentioned before, this requires a strong will and a lot of honesty.

Put an end to your old lies and habits. Sayings like "I like to drink," "I like beer," and "You can still have a drink" are not only inappropriate, they are downright stupid.
These statements are by-products of addiction. They are the "real" devils taking over YOUR life under the alias of "alcohol".
Because alcohol is neutral. It does not care if you become addicted or not.

TWO TYPES OF DEPENDENCE

Generally, people who show signs of failure when withdrawing from their drug are referred to as addicts, and these manifest themselves differently for each person. The person may begin to shake, sweat excessively, freeze, in extreme cases have hallucinations, lose consciousness, or have their organs stop functioning.
As with many things we fear, we put on our blinders.

Out of fear, we dismiss all warning signs that we ourselves may be afflicted with such a disease.

We use exaggerations to make ourselves feel better. These exaggerations are often so highly stylized that we do not notice the real symptoms in ourselves.

So we are out of danger for the time being. After all, we don't tremble and we don't see white mice. Therefore, we are obviously not affected by the disease.

When the first AIDS deaths were announced, everyone cried out: "It can't happen to me. It only happens to gays and junkies!"

At that time, knowledge about the disease was still in its infancy, and only a few people with "extreme" sexual debauchery were known to the public, such as artists, actors, and personalities from the scene.

Dismayed and outraged by the different sexual lives of these people, we demonstrated our pure, untouchable way of life in public.

Although we were perfectly capable of feeling compassion, the condemnation of those affected was initially stronger.
When a disease like AIDS strikes us, we are ostracized by the majority of society.

It is the same with alcoholism. There is no difference at all.

- It is just as deadly in the long run as AIDS.
- It only affects a certain group of people.
  (that's what we think)
- It is just as "image-damaging".

An "exposed" drinker, like an AIDS patient, is also shunned by society because he is equated with the bum on the park bench and thus forced into a role that creates fear.

In the case of the bum, we know that his excessive drinking is to blame for his current situation. And we also drink alcohol.

Therefore, in this case, unlike AIDS, which in the vernacular only affects "gays" anyway, a more complex approach is needed to see through it.

For this purpose, let us first emphasize the symptoms mentioned above, such as the strong trembling, the hallucinations, and let us immediately make these the yardstick for the severity of the disease.

But the accompanying symptoms are actually much more subtle, because addiction can be divided into two categories.

1. psychological addiction
   and
2. physical addiction

Both types of addiction do not necessarily occur together. The physical addiction usually appears later, when the psychological addiction has already affected our lives for a long time.

How quickly one becomes psychologically dependent cannot be generalized. However, the fact is that you are dependent from the moment you start using alcohol specifically and repeat this process at regular intervals.

It usually begins with so-called binge drinking. The reasons for this are usually not obvious. People simply drink to relax. At first, no deviation from what society considers "normal" drinking behavior is noticed.

Slowly but surely, alcohol consumption increases until the person can no longer attend a social event "without" alcohol. Daily life is interspersed with activities that form the basis of rituals.
You have a glass of champagne with breakfast to get your circulation going, a shot of schnapps after a meal to aid digestion. And so on and so forth.

The "psychological" addiction now takes its course and ends, by increasing the dosage of the drink, possibly in physical addiction.
Then the cycle between the two types of addiction is closed.

In addition to the stimulated soul, the body now cries out for the "dearly departed" neurotoxin.
This toxin imperceptibly enters our metabolic system and soon becomes an endogenous substance needed to maintain performance, just like calcium, magnesium, protein, etc.
If you do not give the body the amount it needs, it responds with the symptoms already described, such as trembling, sweating, anxiety, etc.

However, it is not only in the case of physical dependence that we receive a feedback of our disturbed inner balance.
Even in the case of purely psychological addiction, we experience an unpleasant feeling.

If we don't feed our body, i.e. our mind, with alcohol, we become nervous, irritable and literally feel attracted to the bottle.

With no other substance that our body needs to function properly, do we know with such certainty that there is a deficiency. Alcohol is a poison that immediately takes first place in our internal ranking. Once it has taken root, it cries out for gratification, and woe to those who do not yield.

The psychological dependence alone is enough to make our lives a living hell.

The fatal thing about alcoholism is that it is not just the addict's life that is at stake. The behavioral changes caused by the addiction also make life miserable for those around him.

Many react with fear when they realize that others have been harmed by their drinking. They feel guilty. That's why it's so important to take a serious look at addiction and learn about its inner workings. You certainly can't get better with fear. Fear may help you make the decision to stop drinking more quickly.

But in the long run, only a constant maturing process will help.

The realization that the "bums" are at the end of their drinking career and not at the beginning is very sobering. They too started "small". To get down, they had to cut off some branches of their tree of life.

Ignorance and the accompanying attitude of "such a fate cannot touch me" is the beginning of a long, painful descent.

Must it come to this? That is entirely within your power.

I, too, was fortunate in my misfortune. Thank God, not all my worldly achievements went to pieces.

Many of my colleagues and friends didn't even know that I had an alcohol problem. You see, I don't say "had" because the disease is omnipresent even after years of sobriety. An alcoholic remains an alcoholic for life. Don't worry, there really are worse things. The good thing is that you alone can influence whether you stay sober or not.

You are just not "acutely" ill during the dry period, but a tiny sip can change that.

NEVER AGAIN ALCOHOL

This point is unimaginable to many, but for an alcoholic it is a vital foundation.

I am often asked if a small sip would make me dependent again. In order to answer this question adequately, I need to elaborate a bit. It can't be explained in one sentence.

Alcoholics Anonymous is a mental illness to begin with. As the examples described above have shown, we use alcohol because we expect it to have certain effects.

Mental dependence is the beginning of addiction. So I, and I speak for all dry alcoholics, will take great care never to drink a drop again.

This applies to any kind of alcohol. I will not even eat a sauce that I know is flavored with alcohol. However, I have often found out later that alcohol was in the food I had just eaten, and it had no effect on me.

During the drinking period, the oral intake of alcohol becomes a ritual. We know exactly what (intended/desired) effect the intake of alcohol has on our body.

The ritual - "take the bottle, open it, bring it to the mouth, swallow, wait for the effect" - is ingrained in our subconscious.

We inevitably associate each step with the next. Drinking, therefore, is not the actual, natural process of swallowing, but a complex sequence of habits. And these habits become unconscious patterns that we no longer notice even after a short time.

Drinking, and especially the "trappings" that go with it, eventually result in a fixed flow pattern that, after a certain time, forms a certain knitting pattern in our organism - it becomes, so to speak, our second I.

From then on, this second ego takes over in every addict. This extraordinarily egocentric "control organ" looks for the slightest opportunity to seize power in order to eliminate the real, healthy ego.

Even when we feel strong and our will to stop drinking is unbroken, addiction is fighting a very subtle, unfathomable battle that we will not win. We must always be vigilant.

A strong will helps us stop drinking, but knowing the signs of impending relapse helps us stay on track. Never underestimate the disease of addiction.

At this point, imagine the following:

You are a healthy person as long as you are not feeding your alcoholism. As long as your master does not consume alcohol, he is virtually imprisoned in his dungeon. Now, of course, you might say, "The bars behind which I willingly imprison my addiction are solid. He will never get out!"

Of course, you should not be constantly worrying and trembling in fear of this unpleasant cellmate escaping.

But remember, addiction is not "dead"-it is just very patient and has infinite time. And once it has chosen you, it will not let you go.

It just waits for the moment when the jailer gives it a drop, perhaps out of carelessness, because he no longer fears you after a long imprisonment. This drop awakens new strength in the power-hungry prisoner. The addict wants to live, so he does everything he can to behave well so that he is no longer considered dangerous. He hopes to be released from captivity. So be careful not to fall for this game.

I do not want to go into more detail about this now, as I consider the topic of "relapse" to be so important that I have devoted a separate section to it later in the book.

The answer to the earlier question, "Would one drop make me addicted again? "One drop would not make me addicted, because even after a long period of abstinence, I am still addicted. Why should I jeopardize my wonderful life now?"

I can live very well with my "prisoner". I enjoy not having to drink. I feel real compassion for those who still do not want to admit their disease and flush their beautiful, pure ME down the drain with every sip.

I will not judge any of them, because I know how difficult it is to say NO in the beginning. Rather, I will continue to shout encouraging slogans at them, because there is a very valuable prize waiting for everyone who stops valuing alcohol.

Honestly, how long do you want to let an addictive substance control your life? In psychology, the person who does the same thing over and over again, but expects a different result each time, is considered insane.

Can't this be applied to the experience of a drinker? How

many times do you have to wake up in the morning with a thick skull and gaps in your memory before you see through your situation?

THE SEARCH AND ITS OFFERS

Especially with this topic, I will avoid pointing out scientifically proven "blanket symptoms" because I know that, especially in the beginning, people are still looking for "signs" that tell them "you're not really an alcoholic.

My goal is to make you really sensitive to your feelings so that you can actually recognize yourself. I may provoke you occasionally with some of my statements. Perhaps I will have to repeat myself, because just these little provocations can be very helpful, over and over again, in order to achieve an increased depth effect. Please bear with me, it is only to your advantage.

The deeper you think, the more likely you are to get to the bottom of it.

You are an individual. There is no second time for you. Neither in your outer appearance nor in your soul life.

So how is it that there is suddenly absolute agreement among the first messengers of alcoholism? And yet there are some. However, in order for you to be able to use these written documents as profitably as possible, it is necessary for you to look for yourself in them, because they are only similarities.

The psyche also usually plays the key role in the first messengers. We often just have an almost imperceptible desire for a glass.

We do not perceive the deeper reasons. So watch yourself

carefully. Isn't there a small reason that makes you feel "weak" from time to time?

Haven't you been a little angry with your boss? Have you felt inferior in any way to one of your fellow human beings during the day?

Not that you're thinking, "Now he's being oversensitive!"

But my own experiences and my curiosity in talking to people have shown me that it is actually the small, barely perceptible pinpricks that hurt us in our deepest soul and that we do not take seriously and certainly do not talk about because of their supposed unimportance.

Hence my honest question, which I ask you to answer just as honestly:

"Is it possible that you take a drink now and then to ease the pain of these cute little pricks?"

Of course, this doesn't have to apply to you. Just keep reading. Our psyche is a largely unknown, unexplored phenomenon, of whose existence even the most critical of our contemporaries are now convinced, but of whose effects on disease there is equally little experience. Yet the majority of alcoholics agree that this unknown part of our being is largely responsible for the onset of the disease.

We are, therefore, entering uncharted territory that requires extreme caution.

We have the "trails" that many addicts have walked before us and are a living example of a successful expedition.

In order to discuss the first signs of addiction in more detail, I will simply follow these tried and true paths of suffering that have actually occurred, in order to derive new paths from them.

In order to protect the privacy of the people involved, I have limited myself to their first names. Even though all the members of my group are open about their problems, we don't think it makes sense to hang our "suffering" on the big bell. You will learn later why this is so.

Walter F.'s story is a very clear example of how people slowly slip into addiction without realizing it.

Walter F. did not find out when and why he became addicted until after several years of drought.

He was serving his apprenticeship as a locksmith at a time when instructors were still allowed to beat their apprentices. Walter's instructor often took his anger out on him. This was the case on that crucial Friday.

Walter had to endure a lot that day. First beatings, then overtime. When he left the company, his bus had already left and he was standing in the cold. A garage owner near Walter's company was celebrating his birthday at that hour and invited the boy standing in the cold (Walter was 16 at the time) to join him for a beer.

Walter, who had never drunk anything alcoholic before, drank the whole bottle in a short time, not knowing the difference from lemonade.

Just as he had taken his last sip, the next bus arrived.

As he fell into one of the uncomfortable seats, he suddenly felt something great. His fear of the boss was suddenly only half as big. His knees were probably a little weak from the beer, but he felt wonderful.

It was then that addiction began its destructive path. Walter did not have the self-confidence to solve his problems without outside help. No wonder he was a sitting duck.

Of course, the addiction did not take hold of him right away. Walter didn't have to drink himself into unconsciousness.

On the contrary, his thirst for bitter beer was quenched for a long time. But here, too, addiction had the upper hand.

During the next unpleasant encounter with his supervisor, Walter heard a voice from inside himself. He remembered his first beer and the soothing feeling that came over his soul. Then he repeated the process. Again he drank a bottle, and the effect was excellent, as expected.

So he began to use alcohol purposefully, making it his constant companion.

Do you think Walter would have been aware of this danger at the time? After all, he didn't drink every day, and beer didn't taste nearly as good to him as his old-fashioned lemonade.

Today he knows, as do all of us in the group, that anyone who consciously uses alcohol has an alcohol problem, whether he likes it or not. He makes his mental sensations dependent on this means.

At some point, Walter F. was no longer able to get over the slightest inconvenience without taking a drink.

His drinking, which seemed harmless at first, ended after thirty years with a nasty case of pancreatitis. Now, if he wanted to live, he was forced to solve his problems without alcohol.

Lo and behold, it worked. Nothing had changed from when he first got sober. He was still facing his old problems, and new ones were being added every day. He could not visibly improve his life by abstaining from alcohol alone. But he learned to talk about his problems, to find support in a group, and to stop giving power to his addiction.

Walter "needed" a real physical illness to change his life. This was his personal nadir and at the same time the foundation for his new life.

Here it becomes clear that an alcoholic can live unrecognized in an intact society. In Walter's case, fortunately, he had not yet reached the point of social decline. He still had a job and a steady income, and he had never stood out as a drinker because of his already reserved demeanor.

Roland P.'s drinking history was different, although after a long period of abstinence he also recalled that he had initially used alcohol mainly to reduce his shyness towards the opposite sex.
Accordingly, he also used alcohol to achieve a desired state. The reasons why we drink may always be different. The fact that there is a reason remains.
Even then, however, Roland P. found it difficult to control himself, as he told the group. Once he had a beer, it was not easy for him to stop. Tears were the order of the day.
He drank to give himself courage. What he heard from his beloved after many a dance was a deep blow: "You'd be a nice guy if you didn't drink so much.
Irony of fate. Without alcohol he did not dare to approach a girl, with alcohol no one wanted him.
He felt miserable after these experiences. Of course, he suppressed this depression with alcohol again. This went on for many years until he was finally told that his stomach and esophagus were about to burst. The alcohol had completely destroyed the lining. If he had continued to drink, he would most likely have bled to death inside in a very short time.
Since alcoholics are usually sensitive people who are

attached to life, Roland decided to live a life free of addiction. Even after ten years of sobriety, he is still in the group and is grateful that his addiction has given him so much insight.

Monika S.'s drinking career was barely noticeable. For years, she had suffered from low blood pressure, which often left her without energy. On the advice of her family doctor, she drank a glass of champagne every morning.
In fact, the alcohol stimulated her circulation and made her feel good. She also kept to the prescribed amount. Monika S. stuck to her work and did not drink any other alcohol.
It would never have occurred to her to become addicted. But the addiction also found a refuge with her. One day, it was her first vacation day in the Swiss Alps, she found no champagne on the breakfast buffet at the guesthouse.

She began to breathe in a panic, sweating and having an oppressive feeling in her chest. Her pulse was racing and an indescribable feeling of fear tightened in her throat.
Immediately the thought popped into her head, "I need a glass of champagne.
As she felt this thought come to her, she felt ashamed. She concentrated on her breathing, inhaling slowly through her nose and exhaling even more slowly through her mouth. But nothing helped. It was only when she gathered her courage and ordered a bottle of Piccolo from the waitress that her organism calmed down a little. After the first drop, which she swallowed greedily but also fearfully, she suddenly felt better.

But for many years she pushed the idea of addiction aside. It was only after fifteen years of regularly taking this miracle drug that she suddenly found herself at the end of her drinking career.

Nothing worked anymore. One morning, she couldn't get the glass to her mouth. She was shaking so much that she almost spilled everything.

Fearing that she would not be able to get the needed substance into her body, she grabbed the bottle with both hands and greedily drank the entire contents.

Now that her body had calmed down, she knew with absolute certainty that she needed help. She confided in a Blue Cross counselor who immediately advised her to undergo inpatient detoxification followed by therapy (I will talk about detoxification and therapy in more detail later).

Monika remains sober to this day. Certainly, her recovery benefited greatly from her decision to seek professional help.

The course of addiction is different for everyone, but it often ends the same way.

Unfortunately, the end is not always as happy as the drinking careers described above. People who don't recognize their addiction, or don't want to accept that they are addicted, find themselves in the gutter sooner than they would have liked, where they perish, lonely and without warmth.

In order for you to recognize these warning signs in yourself, I will now give you a small list of physical signs that clearly indicate an existing alcohol dependency.

If these symptoms are present, it can be assumed that not only a psychological but also a physical addiction is present. These "signs" do not have to occur in any particular order, nor does this list claim to be exhaustive.

Any one of them alone is indicative of addiction or abnormal drinking behavior and pre-existing physical damage. Likewise, there are no standards for their intensity. Therefore, examine them with the same honesty with which you have answered all previous questions.

- Morning sickness to vomiting
- trembling hands
- shivering of the body (similar to freezing)
- increased nervousness even during
- forced drinking breaks
- sweating
- Sleep disturbances
- Overexcitement
- Need larger quantities
- Suddenly tolerating less
- Cannot stop drinking
- film tear due to alcohol
- Red eyes with a yellowish tint (severe liver damage. See a doctor immediately doctor immediately)
- Pain under right lower rib
- Loss of appetite
- Abnormal weight loss
- Visible blood vessels in the face (facial flushing)
- irregular heartbeat
- Circulation problems
- Increased blood pressure
- Elevated liver enzymes
- Anxiety
- Hallucinations during alcohol withdrawal (life-threatening condition. Call a doctor immediately call a doctor immediately)

- Feeling helpless without alcohol
- You look forward to opportunities to drink (e.g., party, birthday, etc.)
- You look for reasons to justify your drinking
- You cheat about how much you actually drink.
  "I only had two beers". The ten shots are hidden)
  All excuses are found. "I drink because I like drinking". The real reason is hidden. Or
  "I don't like fruit juice. I like beer, etc."
- Secret drinking
- Regular drinking
- Drinking when you feel bad
- Drinking when you feel particularly good
- Binge drinking (can't be for pleasure)
- Drinking and then driving (the desire to drink is already greater than the sense of responsibility)
- general aversion
- work becomes a torture
- frequent minor illnesses are used to stay at home
- minor illnesses are used to feel sorry for oneself. More is drunk
- self-esteem is lowered
- general self-pity. "Nobody likes me
- Personal hygiene is neglected
- Household is neglected
- Invitations from friends are canceled (fear of not getting alcohol)
- Reasons for physical discomfort are faked
- No insight into abnormal drinking behavior
- Changed consciousness (one is no longer the same)

- Tendency to brutality
- You insult your partner
- Unreliability
- etc.

Of course, even people who do not drink alcohol are occasionally overcome by one of these states or emotional movements. These people are not addressed here.

Only those who are at risk of addiction or already addicted due to unusual drinking behavior should feel addressed here. Especially those who live with an unreasonable alcoholic may be able to expose their "Pappenheimer" in this case.

Of course, this exposure should only serve a positive purpose and not drive the addict further into addiction.

To better understand the behavior of a "wet" alcoholic, let us turn to the next point.

THE FLIGHT FORWARD

The worst moment for an alcoholic is when he is exposed by others. Reactions to his involuntary "coming out" vary greatly:

- He denies everything.
- The empty bottles he left everywhere are not his, he says.
- His alcohol fume comes from the "ONE" small glass he just drank.
- He can stop drinking anytime, he says.
- etc.

As a result, he often develops immense willpower. He forces himself not to touch a drop, regardless of all the dangers of radical withdrawal, which is done at home without medical supervision.

Once he has rid his body of the poison, he also feels great again and literally brags about this feat. "You see, I don't need alcohol. What you always think of me".

Amazingly, the addiction hardly bothers him at this stage. He does not feel the slightest desire to take a sip.

He starts to take care of his appearance again, maybe even does some sports, and quickly gains charisma.

In short, he seems to have been miraculously cured. Since his fellow human beings also have little experience with this insidious disease, the world seems to be in order again for everyone.

But beware - this is usually just a phase.

JUST STOPPING DRINKING IS NOT ENOUGH!

Now you may be thinking, "He's not happy with anything! He said himself that if you're an alcoholic, you can't drink anymore!" That's true, but I also said that you need more than just a strong will to achieve lasting abstinence.

Namely, a sound knowledge of how this addictive disease works.

It is during these brief periods of sobriety, often called relapses out of ignorance (we will discuss real relapses in Chapter 4), that the addict loses an enormous amount of self-esteem.

Because, unfortunately, after several weeks of evidence, he is all too thirsty. He has dethroned the addiction that is already firmly entrenched in his psyche. It no longer appears to him as THE great danger, "as he was led to believe.

After all, he has proven that he can stop drinking whenever he wants. What the hell does he have to do with addiction now? At first glance, it even sounds plausible.

He has triumphed over his addiction, even if only for a short time. But this is where the disease comes into play. The addiction has once again shown its best side. It has given in to his desire to be the master of the house. She has shown herself defeated and has given him her full admiration.

And he, in the supposed spotlight of success, like an aging, vain actor who hasn't been asked for an autograph in years, has allowed himself to be celebrated by his "only fan" as a brave, irrefutable hero.

The addiction in this case was the cunning fox and he was the simple-minded hare, and he fell for it completely. The hare opened the fox's cage and jumped back in.

Unfortunately, I have opened the bars often enough myself and know what a sweet way the fox can be. So I can say with certainty that we must always be on guard against such flattery.

It is all too understandable, given our image of the "real drinker," that we want to avoid being labeled as such at all costs.

No wonder we run away and fight it with all our might. But as long as we give alcohol this high status, the game will be played over and over again.

Addiction will also figure out how to reclaim its territory, and it is far more experienced than we will ever be. Now, you may think this sounds like a split personality, and that's exactly what it is. An alcoholic becomes a proxy for his addiction and is unable to control it. It is amazing how deeply the disease burrows into our psyche. It wants to win at all costs and keeps making up new rules of the game that, by the time we understand them, have long since been changed.

If addiction senses the slightest headwind, it cancels its sails immediately. It does not want to be seen as a "parasite". It is afraid that you will free yourself from it and thus deprive it of its existence.

You see, we are indeed walking on very thin ice. But the ice will support us if we trust those who have proven to us that alcohol has no place in our lives. These people know the path that leads across that thin layer of ice.

Addiction will always try to draw you out. It will make itself as small as a mouse. Barely perceptible, it will nest inside you. If the nest were in your house, you would call an exterminator to drive out the brood for good. In your case, you have to do it yourself.

And that means, in plain English, "Stop fooling yourself and others!

Stop thinking that alcohol is the meaning of life. Look at the faces of those who get drunk all the time.

Do you have respect for them? No, then why should anyone respect you when you've poured yourself another one?

What the hell is so nice about constantly running the risk of putting your life in the hands of a power-hungry, self-centered beast? Take your life into your own hands.

Get rid of the idea that alcohol is part of life.

Why don't you be open with the people you love and not lie to them all the time?

You don't deserve to be seen as a liar. Just as those around you do not deserve to be lied to by you.

What could be more beautiful than looking your children or

your precious partner in life clearly and soberly in the eye?

It is a wonderful feeling when you can look deeply and honestly into each other's eyes. There is nothing more beautiful than the love that comes out.

Put yourself in the position of what it must feel like to be approached by your partner, father, or mother with an unpleasant smell of alcohol.

As a member of this society, as a parent, and as a partner in a relationship, you now have a certain responsibility. And if you cannot handle that responsibility, seek help and you will find it.

You are not the only one who has problems. But if you continue to resign yourself to the fact that your addiction, for which no one will hold you responsible if you do something about it, will control the rest of your life, you may soon find yourself all alone.

I don't mean to scare you, but never underestimate the tenacity of the offended.

The alcohol problem does not affect you alone, although it is all too human to wallow in self-pity alone, but alcoholism is a partnership problem.

Every alcoholic inevitably drags those around him down with him. If he loses his job because of his drinking, his family goes to the dogs with him.

But the most important reason to put the alcohol beast behind bars once and for all is you.

You have the right to live a free, fulfilling life without restrictions. Even if you live alone, without a family, you deserve to pursue your hobbies and pleasures unhindered.

We are all born free and independent individuals. Slavery

was abolished long ago.

We are the masters of our lives and no one has the right to manipulate our health.

If you continue to let addiction take over, you are enslaving yourself and robbing yourself of your personal freedom.

To learn true freedom, imagine yourself in wonderful situations as often as possible.

Visualize moments when you are confidently, naturally, and calmly overcoming problems that before you could only have endured in a drunken stupor.

Then feel intensely the respect shown to you and always remember: "First was the thought.

If you have to take a few low blows in the course of the day, look for positive side effects in those low blows that can benefit you in the future.

Every experience that seems negative at first glance contains an opportunity for personal growth.

It is of the utmost importance for any alcoholic to take a hard look at the positive things in life.

This takes some intense training at first, but like everything else in life, it can be learned.

Everything has two sides. It depends which side you want to live on. As long as you give alcohol the slightest importance, you will not be able to really think positively because you will always be looking for a reason to get drunk.

Be sure to look for daily reasons why life without this drug is much more valuable.

Think about the person you will be then. A person who rests in himself and is ready to absorb daily new knowledge that will help him grow out of the alcohol problem and not break from it.

A very nice man in my group, who has been sober for many years, once told me about a conversation he had with his pastor shortly after he began his sobriety, at a time when he had not yet come to terms with his decision.

The gist of the conversation was this: "Father, why did this disease strike me of all people?" To which the priest replied, "God must love you immensely to have given you this chance!"

Admittedly, it is not easy to understand the truth behind these words, but yes, it is indeed an opportunity that only comes to a person who masters this problem. I am sure you will know this by the end of this book.

ALCOHOLICS ARE THE BEST ACTORS

Once the addict recognizes his abnormal drinking behavior, he truly "puts on the mask," just as an actor does before a performance. There he puts on the appropriate face he needs for the particular social performance.

His big performance begins. A "play" about life and death, about good and evil. His antennae are now very sensitive.

He sees in every little utterance concerning his person an attack on his life and is deeply offended.

In this stage of dependence, he is like a mimosa. Because of his attitude and way of thinking, he becomes more and more marginalized.

"Just don't blow your cover" is the motto.

He can literally hear the grass grow. It takes a lot of strength to downplay the addiction and act normal. And no one must notice that he is acting according to his "inner script.

He rewrites that script every day. But since he lacks a prompter to whisper the constantly changing text to him, he often drinks even more to stay calm.

Only when he has had the necessary amount does he

become a little more confident.

Of course, it also depends on his personality, whether he is naturally shy or rather cheeky.

Many are even extremely confident at this stage and turn the tables on others:

"Who cares if I drink or not? I can do whatever I want. This This "drinker type" often has a hard time letting his problem out, because by nature he embodies the tough, no-nonsense contemporary.

We find this characteristic in both men and women. The signs and behaviors are often the same. It is just that we find women less often at the regulars' table, where this type of man is often the leader.

At the regulars' table, the man who can hold his liquor is still a real man. Here, he's not reprimanded for his behavior if he's had one too many. On the contrary, people here want to see achievement.

So he begins to measure himself by the standards that prevail there.

He then accepts this measure as "normal" and even reduces his existing alcohol problem in the short term. His conscience is appeased for the time being.

Because of his intransigent behavior, this type can only be stopped in practice by physical illness or an angry supervisor.

"You're going to rehab or you're fired!" Since he desperately needs the money for his dissolute life, he actually puts himself in the hands of a health resort. But instead of insight, he gets more knowledge to better cover up his "alleged" illness in the future. At the very least, he sees this short-term abstinence as further proof that his quiet realization that he might have an alcohol problem is pure fantasy.

His biggest problem is the high status of this social drug. Even if he suffers many setbacks at this stage, he will only look for reasons to justify his drinking.

This "stubbornness" is very often shown by more sensitive people when they realize that alcohol is indeed a problem for them, but they don't know or can't imagine a life "without" it.

Even the certainty that their strange drinking habits might one day lead them to the bottom of the barrel does not stop them from continuing to drink.

It is precisely this certainty that causes them to exaggerate the whole thing. They fear an alcohol-free future. How will they cope with their problems without a drink?

So they give up inside and return to the stage and the macabre play with the title "We drink ourselves to death and tear down all those who are close to us".

It is terrible what you go through in this phase. You know that other people live clean, reliable lives, and you think that your own inability to do the same is a weakness or a punishment imposed by God.

Self-loathing then becomes a destructive act of struggle in which, unfortunately, the people who love us also perish.

"How could anyone mean well for me?" is often the dominant thought. The drinker does not agree with himself, yet he justifies his behavior every day.

When his partner says, "You drink too much," he just smirks arrogantly. "What do you know about me? I drink because I enjoy it," is the standard response.

Of course, the answer varies from "type" to "type. The resolute one will answer as above, while the more sensitive one might say, "Otherwise I can't stand the pressure that's being put on me.

Now you can see for yourself that it depends on your personal attitude whether you want to do the big show to perfection or whether you prefer to get help. I must admit that I have often sought help, but due to my wife's ignorance about alcoholism, I have never been able to get any real help. Her answers to my questions were probably sincere, but they only made me more painfully aware of my inadequacy, which in turn led to further escapades.

The inventiveness of the alcoholic is limitless. Revealing himself to his partner, whose answers inadvertently bring him further shame, possibly plunging him into even deeper depression.

To avoid looking like a weakling in the future, he plays an even more perfidious game. He becomes cynical, insulting, and humiliating to his helpful partner in order to elevate himself a bit.

As long as he maintains his alcohol level, he enjoys this role to the fullest. When the level drops and his feelings of guilt and shame return, he continues to drink.

This drinking may even take place in public, but will be demonstratively limited.

He may make sure to take something nonalcoholic after the third drink to deliberately punish his partner. His efforts are now directed solely at revenge for the vile insinuations made against him. He is clearly in control.

This behavior is a real "brain or personality doping" for him. He catapults himself to the throne of a despot.

No wonder that he soon becomes lonely in this role and that his audience, an "inferior" foot race, no longer laughs at his jokes.

It can take a long time for him to give up his hard "drowned" status. Often by then the marriage is broken and friendships are shattered.

When he becomes aware of his loneliness, he falls completely into the abyss. Either he finally wakes up or he pretends to ask for forgiveness.

"I solemnly promise you that I won't drink anymore!" If your partner agrees, and possibly makes further demands, say "Yes" and "Amen" ruefully.

At this point, he must realize once again what a weakling he is. Addiction enjoys its position of power especially at this time. Under no circumstances will it give up its victim without a fight.

On the one hand, the addict doesn't want to jeopardize his partnership; on the other hand, the pressure of the addiction is growing. How is he supposed to do it all?

He is completely overwhelmed. But what about talking to the partner, who now thinks that everything will be fine and that he has the alcohol problem under control?

Who can help now?

And this is what the disease has been waiting for. It is preparing him for a new battle, and that battle is called concealment.

SECRETLY UNCANNY

In order to make real progress, you should always remember that you may not be able to transfer absolute matches of the processes and behaviors described to yourself.

It would be impossible to extract every detail from an army of drinkers. Much more valuable are the positive impulses that victory over addiction is very much on the agenda and by no means impossible.

Precisely because secret drinking takes place in our deepest intimacy, many can only talk about it openly and honestly after years. Some never come out because they are still ashamed.

But I promise not to mince words, whether it is about my life or that of my willing interlocutors.

Secret drinking was and is the most interesting topic for me after my drinking career. It is unimaginable how sick alcohol can make you.

Drinkers come up with the most outrageous ideas to hide their drinking from the public.

After some time of sobriety, however, you can laugh heartily about your deeds. It makes you really happy to know that you have broken the power of addiction. The addiction is responsible for a change in personality that sometimes manifests itself in grotesque ways. I call my former self "Dr. Jekyll and Mr. Hyde.

I really had two faces, with Mr. Hyde dominating quite early on. When I think about the fact that I drank alcohol for the first time when I was about 20 years old, and what it turned into over the next twelve years, I can only answer very seriously: "People, beware of the devil in the form of an angel.

Back then, when I took my first sip, my knees immediately went weak and my surroundings began to spin.

Many of my friends at that time could already drink properly. It was not uncommon for me to hear: "Man, what a wimp you are. You can't even drink a beer without falling over. My self-confidence was not very strong at that time, so this hit me like a thunderbolt. I, the born athlete, became an outsider because of my healthy lifestyle. I wanted to show them.

I was stupid enough to sit down in my parents' living room in the evening and slowly drink a beer for "training purposes".

The effect was disastrous. My "clean" organism fought with all its might against this poison. I felt sick and had to vomit.

"I guess the others are right," I thought, and continued training with all my ambition.

I also had no "sober" role models in my family. Everyone drank alcohol. And they were all respectable people with a certain social status.

I wanted to be like them. Eventually, I was able to hold my own at the bar.

As my tolerance for alcohol grew, so did my esteem. Suddenly I was one of them.

Of course, at that time I could not see that before, because of my athletic and clean lifestyle, they silently envied me.

The respect they showed me afterwards was only the result of their successful strategy of equality. They had brought me up to their level without having to work on themselves.

But you have to see through that first. When I reaped the rewards of my relentless efforts a few years later, I was horrified to discover that some of the "culprits" had long since stopped drinking, others were probably still drinking without being addicted, and a few were going through the same thing I was.

But they were only comforting for a short time. I wanted to measure myself again against those who had stopped drinking.

But these friends wanted nothing more to do with me. But in order to be respected again in their circle, I began to drink secretly.

On the outside I was the old sportsman again, but on the inside I was a desperate addict.

I drank in the car. I drank in the basement. I drank at night when my wife was asleep. The addiction now took all my strength.

To get through the "stress" (there were many reasons) at work, I put an iron ration under the driver's seat. More and more often I would sneak out of the office to refuel.

I was no longer hungry. I got all my nutrients from cognac and champagne. What had started so harmlessly with a beer now cost a fortune, accompanied by a steadily declining quality of life.

Then there were the countless breath improvers, such as chewing gum and menthol candies, which I still suck today, but only to prevent possible garlic fumes.

At the beginning of my dryness, I didn't dare to use these sweets for a long time because I was afraid that people around me would draw the wrong conclusions. But with time, you get over certain things.

You see how mentally confused one can become.

Back to the subject.

Secret drinking is actually the result of the behavior of those close to us.

They constantly forbid us to drink or at least control the amount we drink. It bothers us to be constantly reminded of our addiction.

So we drink in such a way that they no longer notice. They see that we are making an effort to drink less, and we (perhaps) gain a little respect from them.

"Tricked," we laugh inwardly, not realizing that the addiction's strategy is far better than our mind's, and that the addiction is the one that has reason to smile.

We don't realize that we are just puppets.

After all, life consists only of an ever-improving replenishment plan. We think, plan and act according to the desires of our addiction and do not realize how far away we are from real life.

This secret drinking requires an enormous amount of strength, strength that you don't really have at this stage.

Since the addiction completely dominates us at this stage and constantly reminds us that we cannot live without the substance we demand, we are in a kind of death throes.

All available reserves are mobilized.

Due to this high physical stress, we are completely "pumped out". Now, in many cases, the effect of alcohol hits like a bomb. The result is that even with alcohol nothing works, but without it we "can't" either.

We have now reached a point where, out of pure survival instinct, we prescribe ourselves the poison from the bottle. The supply must never run out, otherwise inner peace is over.

Secret drinking is taken to perfection. It is no longer enough to deceive family and friends, but all the people we meet every day.

Through my interlocutors I have heard of such perfidious methods, carried out with enormous conviction, that Hollywood would give an Oscar for them any day.

I will tell you some stories that a "sane" person would consider a very good joke.

One man in my support group bought three newspapers and three bitters at the newsstand every day during his secret drinking phase.

At first glance, there is nothing wrong with this. "He's just a very helpful person who thinks of his co-workers," you might say.

But unfortunately, he was not nice at all, but unspeakably sick. He threw two newspapers into the garbage can and then drank the three bitters by himself.

That way he got the ration he needed without looking suspicious. The kiosk owner increased his newspaper sales, and the poor guy got his "elixir of life" inconspicuously.

Another was drunk as a skunk every night after work. "We never see him drinking," his colleagues said, "and yet he is always drunk at the end of the day.

Only after a long period of abstinence did he reveal his secret. He was eating kilos of oranges. "So what, that's healthy," we say. "Of course," but if you inject the citrus fruits with high-proof liquor and eat ten of them a day, they also have their effect.

The wife of another alcoholic was at a loss for words. She watched her husband's every move. She turned the entire apartment, garage, and gazebo upside down. Nowhere were bottles or other containers to be found.

And yet, after a day of gardening, he was drunk. She thought that maybe his body was not breaking down the alcohol and he was under constant power.

In the end, she could find no plausible explanation. Again, the mystery was not solved until many years later.

The beds and paths of the garden were littered with empty bottles. You know how it is, you stick empty bottles head first into the ground so that the shape of each bed remains clearly outlined.

Unfortunately, her husband regularly replaced the empty bottles with full ones to keep the supply going. This way, he could quench his thirst at a moment's notice without his wife suspecting anything.

Sneaking water into empty bottles is an old trick. The more "exotic" methods, however, have a much greater appeal.

Like that of a housewife who had been drinking for years, much to the chagrin of her husband. She hung the bottles on a rope out of the window. No matter how many times he checked the apartment, there was no alcohol in the house, and she still slurred her words in the evening. But this is a trick that a sane person would not think of.

Another woman who shared the apartment with a friend also came up with something very special. She killed two birds with one stone. The bottles could never be found, and it kept them cool. She stashed her rations in the toilet cistern.
She probably would not have been discovered if she had emptied her secret reservoir every once in a while.
But when the box was filled to the brim with empties, there was no room for the actual contents.
The plumber called by the friend burst the bomb. It was an embarrassing end that made the victim look for more sophisticated methods.

The trick with the thermos flask containing cold liquor instead of hot coffee is nothing new either.

But turning the entire interior of a car dashboard into a flask depot is much more attractive.
It took an accident to discover the inventor of this original fuel depot. The hard impact broke the car body and a lot of empty bottles were scattered on the road.
A blood test revealed that the driver had a blood alcohol level of 3.5. Unfortunately, this incident was not enough to make him think about his drinking habits. He continues to drink happily to this day, fooling his friends and most of all himself, probably without a license, but that's about it.
Some people never learn until it is too late.

Other depots are often called flower vases, watering cans, Leitz folders and even mailboxes.

You would not believe how many bottles fit into a mailbox. Also, this place is relatively safe from unauthorized access. However, you have to take the spare key with you so that your partner doesn't "stupidly" get the mail.

But no matter how careful you are, the impossible can still happen. The person in question told me that he once lost his key while drunk, and his wife, delighted by its sudden appearance, finally went to get the mail herself.

The bottles fell towards her with a loud roar and shattered on the floor, whereupon he heard

heard cursing in his sleep.

The house was in a very bad state that day.

Despite their amusing entertainment value, these stories have, of course, a very sad background. No director would ever come up with such crazy ideas.

Maybe this will help people who live with an alcoholic to get behind their game and not constantly doubt themselves and their fears and observations.

Because it often happens to every alcoholic that his experiences simply do not seem real to him. He is simply unable to think as sickly as the addict does and must.

Therefore, in the next part, I will show all CO's how best to behave by gaining insight into the secret bag of tricks of the alcoholic.

THE ROLE OF THE CO-ALCOHOLIC

This group of people plays a key role in the career of every alcoholic.

He suffers torment that he rarely can, and often will not,

confide in anyone.

This is understandable. For he, too, has a certain image of the alcoholic, as described at the beginning. He also does not want to admit that his partner is a "real" addict and that his behavior is determined by his addiction.

I have heard of very serious fates, and I really feel sorry for these co-alcoholics. They watch helplessly as the person they once loved perishes because of excessive drinking. It is not only the destruction of the addict himself that is so tragic. No, the fact that the addiction destroys the whole togetherness is far worse.

The addict takes advantage of his partner whenever and wherever he can. He makes them his sidekick and, unfortunately, all too often his enforcer.

The co-alcoholic is the one who has the drinker's back. He makes his coffee the next morning after a night of drinking, he does his share of the housework, and he lies for him when he is unable to fulfill his obligations.

The spouse has his or her hands full trying to spoon out the soup that the addicted partner has gotten them into.

Since none of us wants to admit that someone in our own family has such a hideous, "humiliating" disease, we do everything we can to suppress its existence and eventually cover it up.

Has anyone ever had a problem saying, "My husband or wife has diabetes"? No, even though the disease is a perfect comparison. Those who have diabetes are not allowed to eat sugar and other sweetened foods.

Also, just like alcoholism, diabetes is a disease that accompanies us throughout our lives.

Like alcoholism, diabetes is a lifelong disease that cannot be cured; it can only be controlled by a healthy lifestyle and, in this case, by taking insulin. Just as drunkenness is prevented by a lifelong abstinence from alcohol.

And yet, a diabetic receives more sympathy than an alcoholic, even though both are diseases that no one intentionally brings upon themselves. But we see how differently society reacts. So you should stand up right away. Start educating yourself, as a fellow sufferer, about your partner's disease. You can go to many groups to get the knowledge you need.

Groups like the Blue Cross, Alcoholics Anonymous, the Good Templars, and many others will be happy to take you in. Even or especially fellow alcoholics can get help there at any time.

Al-Anon is a self-help group specifically for alcoholics. Do not tell your partner where you are going. You may make things worse than they need to be.

Although I strongly recommend that you join a group, as does the addict himself, I would like to give you some food for thought that may make the beginning a little easier.

Only when you know how to act can you safely go on the offensive.

It may seem strange at first to call your partner an alcoholic, but you will soon realize how many of those around you already knew it, just never said it to you.

First, think about the time of drought. How wonderful it will be when you can enjoy life "together" again. Realize once and for all that only stopping the addiction can change the current situation.

Make no compromises. Judge your partner's drinking by "normal", healthy standards.

No one has the right to mess with your life. Of course, it is love for your partner that has caused you to take on this problem.

Do everything you can to get rid of this problem. But do not forget your own future. There is only one way to achieve your goal. And that is abstinence, no ifs or buts. Do not get involved in any "games". Choose the successful way. And you will only be able to walk this path permanently if you get the necessary information and then implement it constantly. This means that you also have to learn how to deal with addiction, because addiction has changed you in ways that you may not realize at the moment.

Every addict inevitably drags his or her personal environment down with them. Those around you have only one serious disadvantage: they are aware of all the details of the addiction and usually suffer even more than the addict.

First, you must break out of your prison. Open up to your partner's addiction and stop making a fool of yourself for him.

From now on, you have to take over the thinking, because for him, only the addiction thinks, and for him, only the satisfaction of the addiction. And all means are right for him. Even the use of YOUR life.

What is at stake for you? The addict doesn't care what happens to him as long as he is functioning.

Show him clearly that you will no longer be used in this way and for the purpose of satisfying the addiction. You have to be very, very consistent.

The addict has an above-average sense of perception that will alert him to every little hole in his defense system. He will shamelessly exploit any small concession or sign of indecision on your part to strengthen his position.

So avoid empty threats, because he will see through them very quickly. How many times have you packed your bags, only to have him take you back and put your clothes back neatly in the closet? Show him clearly that you are no longer joking with him. The best way to do this is to stop doing work that directly supports the addiction.

Leave him alone to deal with the effects of the addiction. Make it clear to him how difficult it is to overcome the side effects of his drinking.

In good English, "let him lie in his vomit until he has slept off his intoxication. Make sure that he lies properly and does not suffocate, so that he can wake up without major damage in his stinking "waste products" and feel what you have done for him so far. Make him his own teacher through such lessons. This is the quickest way for him to realize how disgusting addiction really is. He needs to feel on his own body that you mean business. Now pack your bags "for good" and move in with friends for a few days. Telling them what you are going through will make you feel lighter. But don't expect a lot of understanding right away. Remember that your experiences will not be received by outsiders with the same intensity that you feel every day.

You need a lot of strength right now. On the one hand, you have to deal with the humiliations of the past few years, and on the other, you may have to contend with the possible ignorance of your fellow human beings.

I can only encourage you at this point. There are more fellow sufferers than you might think at the moment. But the step to freedom, no matter how difficult it may be, is the only right one. Imagine what will happen if he continues to drink.

Loss of job, social security, physical and mental deterioration, a life on the edge. Not only do you help your sick partner, but you also have a unique opportunity to start over.

This requires absolute honesty. And the quickest way to achieve this honesty is to tell the truth from now on, and to stop making up euphemistic excuses for his illness. For these excuses are proof that you, too, are basically mentally ill.

A Mr. Hyde has also been living inside you for a long time, just waiting to subjugate the real you.

Because the co-alcoholic's "unknowing" behavior often helps the addiction take root in the entire family, he or she is very slow to realize that significant personality changes are taking place in the immediate family as well.

Everything revolves around him. Even though he is no longer able to fulfill his obligations, he plays first fiddle. His family is afraid to talk to him about his problem because he might "snap" again, or at least turn the tables and reward the concerned person with a barrage of profanity. In many cases, there is no communication within the family.

People avoid personal conversations for fear of further disappointment, and try with all their might to represent the "ideal world" to the outside world.

One simply does not want to admit that one's whole life is being destroyed or is already being destroyed. Many co-alcoholics therefore take refuge in a dream world. In effect, they pretend that everything is perfectly normal.

For this reason, it is all too understandable that the addict lies when his or her partner's boss calls: "My husband, my wife can't come to work today. He/she has the flu".

From now on, don't give Mr. Hyde a chance to triumph. Begin to take responsibility for yourself and your partner by stating the real reasons for his or her inability to work: "My husband/wife is drunk in bed. He/she cannot come to work". Nowadays, most employers prefer sober employees because they are more reliable. So the next time you call or talk to your boss, tell him what's going on with your partner and ask for his help. He should address your partner's addiction. Again, a consistent approach is essential.

Either get him into treatment or threaten to fire him.

His boss may even be grateful because he has been happy with his performance and does not want to lose him.

So not only are you doing your partner a favor, but you are also doing your part to improve his productivity, which will make the boss happy rather than angry.

Now he is faced with a decision that awaits a clear answer.

In most cases, it takes outside pressure for the addict to come to his senses. But again, I can tell you from experience that the majority of addicts are happy to finally get help, knowing that they will not be thrown out on the street.

He has the support of his partner and his company. With this sense of security, he can concentrate fully on his recovery.

In therapy, his body is first freed from the poison and he has the opportunity to rethink his life in a safe environment. Once the mind is free of alcohol and its availability for a while, the "awakening" begins in most cases. So give him that chance. What do you have to lose? If he decides to continue drinking despite all the external pressure, YOUR life will have no ups, either. So why not make a clear decision right now?

If he does not want to be helped, he must surrender to his self-imposed fate.

Then at least you will have done your best, and you will not have to blame yourself. But if you just sit back and watch, you will both go to the dogs. And you will have nothing left.

You may hear your parents-in-law and friends blaming you for not helping him and for not asking for help. In the end, you may be blamed for his death.

So start today to stand up for YOUR future and that of your partner, because without your help he may have no future. As long as he is drinking, he is living in the past and his present life is lived by his addiction.

Do not blame him for his disease. Help him recognize himself and show him that he has the opportunity to become the person he once was.

You can only do this by showing him that it is possible without alcohol. If you have been drinking with him from time to time, stop.

Show him clearly that you love him and want to stay with him, but not on his terms.

Do not behave toward him as he expects you to behave in your role as a reliable CO. Constantly hold up a mirror to him. However, the tips I give you should be taken with a grain of salt. If your partner is prone to fisticuffs, you should think of his personal safety first.

So don't provoke him too much, or better yet, observe his actions from a safe distance until he sobers up.

My experience has shown that all alcoholics rely on their CO one hundred percent. The CO is watchdog, nurse, and pastor all in one.

Show him by your behavior that this will no longer be the case. Stop quietly buying alcohol as if it were a normal part of your household.

If he is thirsty, let him get it himself. If he insists that you go, then buy him something. The wife of a group member reported that one day she took a very drastic measure. When she went to get him vodka from the gas station, as he had requested, she immediately slammed two bottles down on the table and said, "Here, drink yourself to death. But hurry up!"

She let him know with all her heart that she didn't care what happened to him. In this case, her reaction actually had an effect. Her harsh words woke him up and he actually stopped drinking.

It is not enough just to confront him about his drinking. What he needs to know is that you are no longer willing to let alcohol destroy your life.

If your words make him get loud, open all the doors and windows so the neighbors can hear what's going on in your apartment. You will be surprised at how quickly he will calm down.
He doesn't want to draw attention to himself.

If he continues to drink after your "warnings", you will literally leave him in a pool of vomit. The next morning, he will look stupidly out of the laundry when you are gone.

You should start all your efforts to get him off alcohol only when he is sober anyway, because when he is drunk he is not his own master and then the addiction determines his actions.

So your core message must always be: "I don't care if you destroy your life. I will not let you destroy mine.
Do not miss any opportunity to participate in real life again. If you feel like going to the movies, the opera, or anywhere else, go. Live as if you were already free.
If on such an occasion you are asked why you came alone, you know that your answer can only be: "He/she is drunk again.
You are responsible for your own life, so act responsibly. Do not cover up your addicted partner's behavior in front of your children. Tell them what is going on.
The children need to know with absolute certainty that you are not to blame for the strange behavior of their father or mother.
There is nothing worse for children than secrecy. Because then they also flee into a world that is out of touch with reality.

"My mother/father is sick. Tell the teachers and the children what is really going on. Don't let your children be raised to be co-conspirators.

They are innocent and do not deserve to be burdened with a history that will destroy their future. With your honest education, they will learn the consequences of using this drug.

It's not that they won't end up hitting the bottle for the rest of their lives as a result of this education. But they are more likely to understand that alcoholism is a disease for which there is nothing to be ashamed of. It will not be a taboo subject in your family, and it will not be swept under the rug, as it was in previous generations and still is in much of the population today.

Free yourself from all the stereotypes about alcoholism. You can be proud of your courage and honesty, and you will earn nothing but respect from all sides.

If you maintain your current role, YOU may not be saved either.

As mentioned before, for a long time the disease takes place exclusively in the psyche. And it is the psyche that is heavily burdened in the alcoholic. Even the strictest advocates of orthodox medicine today agree that many physical illnesses have their roots in an ailing soul.

The fear of becoming physically ill should not be at the center of our thinking. We can enjoy everything intensely when our mind is healthy. Perhaps the mind is indeed the part that makes us what we are, sentient, empathic beings.

If the true basis of our existence is the soul, then it is obvious that we must first make sure that we are free from constraints.

Today, I can also say with full conviction that it was not so much the physical impairments during my time of drinking that were a torment, but rather my destroyed soul that caused me trouble. I was no longer able to see the world around me with all its beauty and problems. I was a slave to this evil drug whose chains paralyzed my unique diversity.

The now recovered, healthy psyche allows me to be free today. Not that I look at life through rose-colored glasses, but rather that I experience daily joy in solving everyday tasks that had stood in my way like tons of rocks when I was drinking.

Life must be turned into a competition. Give your best with fun and energy, with the Olympic resolution "to be there is everything.

As a recovering alcoholic, do you see your current role primarily as one of bringing alcohol down from its current status?

There is nothing better than a clear mind and soothing relaxation with a good cup of tea.

Perhaps I can give you some food for thought on this subject to help you deal with your problems with your partner.

Read on and put yourself in the addict's shoes. This will help you better understand his behavior and realize that he can't help it.

This insight will also help you optimize your strategy.

LIFE BECOMES TORTURE

The behavior of the now-informed co-alcoholic begins a real gauntlet for the addict.

The daily signals he receives prove his inadequacy. It would be too easy for him to stop drinking immediately after a few "nasty" remarks from his partner.

At this point in a drinker's career, a fight to the death usually begins anew. The mirror held up to him again and again shows his ugliest face.

Seeing that "strange", disgusting face every morning, he vows never to take another sip. "I'll show them".

Too often, however, it remains only a vow. The addiction is stronger. It demands its

right. It determines what is drunk, not the person affected by it.

And again the addict gives in, because he is already going through hell from the short withdrawal, which he again interprets as weakness.

Very often this results in a spatial escape. The addict is ashamed to go home, so he prefers to stay in some pub until curfew to make sure his partner is asleep until he arrives. He consciously avoids personal contact.

The words of his family and friends are omnipresent. Not only does his bathroom mirror tell him the truth to his face, no, all the people who live sober, addiction-free lives literally hold the knife to his throat.

He is lonely. Feelings of shame and a very strong sense of inferiority prevent him from interacting with people of his social class.

He is still unable to ask these same people for help. Alcohol continues to take over.

He has a strong desire to be a strong, confident, successful person. However, his mirror and all other external remarks tell him that he is just a drunk, unable to cope with his problems.

He can no longer bear the torment and is looking for ways out that offer him less painful results. He wants to be a whole man who is considered a man despite his drinking.

Who now supports him in his pathological belief that he can be the man he wants to be even when he is drunk?

The answer is obvious. People much deeper in addiction and far below his level.

From now on, he spends his time in rundown bars where only "subjects" of alcoholism frequent.

Bums, social failures. Here he is suddenly king again. There he is somebody again. With his financial power still intact, he is generous and quickly gains prestige.

In short, he feels like a million bucks again. In this environment, he may still refer to his former friends as "arrogant idiots" and thus get a good laugh from his new interlocutors.

His previous conviction of being a failure is transformed into a very "social" approach to life that has brought him into these "humble circles. He makes it clear to his attentive "friends" what a great job he has and how generous he is.

He becomes more and more absorbed in the new dream world, not realizing that these are the harbingers of his descent.

Through the respect of his drinking companions, he blossoms into a new beauty. At least while he is drinking.

Only in the morning does he look in the mirror. "Nothing is eaten as hot as it is cooked" is his new motto.

From his throne he calls all his opponents "worms" who can't really hold a candle to him.

The period he is now going through will prove to be a real test of all personal relationships.

Many of his otherwise loyal friends and family members are now understandably turning away from him. After all, he does not have a good word for them.

Perhaps his current attitude even gives him a sense of

power, which he enjoys, over the pain threshold of those affected.

He thinks he has the situation under control and drinks more than ever.

The initial torment becomes a virtue. Hard-drinking men are crowned heroes, men who don't drink are declared wimps. The solution to one's drinking problem lies in the idea of increasing one's drinking and thus finally becoming the star of the drinking scene. What is the meaning of life? Are those who are always sober and responsible with themselves and others right, or those who know how to "enjoy" properly? Suddenly, the undeniable addiction is a pleasure.

His whole value system is shaken.

Nothing that was important to him before he started drinking is important now. Alcohol becomes even more important, or rather, it becomes the basis of life, the meaning of existence. His "life script" gets a new content and punishes all the dear, caring people with lies.

When this view becomes the drinker's philosophy of life, all duties and obligations become secondary.

He is sure that everyone only cares about him because they are interested in his monthly income.

"Yes, exactly, it's all their fault. They just took advantage of me and made me drink. He has finally found the culprits. Now he's going to take revenge. "They will see what they have in me.

EVERYTHING EVERYWHERE

Again, I note that this behavior does not apply to all addicts, but many of my interviewees reported thinking this way.

It is all too human for an addict to reject blame. It is the addict who is unable to take responsibility for his actions.

The disease is also far too persistent to give in. It makes the addict believe that he is the master of the situation. The addiction absorbs all expressions of the caring partner and sets the course in time.

It thwarts any semblance of reason. Its will to survive is very strong. The addiction demands absolute loyalty. When it has reached the point where the addicted person stands in front of it, it whispers confidence in his ear with the tongues of angels.

It is not the addiction that is responsible for his condition, but his environment that has brought him to where he is today. With all his might, he stands up for his inner tormentor without even thinking that the addiction might have something evil in mind.

Only society is guilty and condemned. You yourself are only the victim of scheming people who have insidiously crept into your life.

All friends who sincerely sympathize with you are considered to be false, selfish subjects.

Why in God's world should he still play along? Isn't it true that only cheats and unscrupulous people get anywhere in life? Doesn't a decent person have the worse cards to begin with? These thought processes are often very pronounced in the addict and therefore determine all his actions.

He feels sorry for his situation and hates anyone who seems to live carelessly. He sees his situation as God's fate. His drinking is a kind of defiant reaction to all the punishments imposed on him.

Only those who put their lives in the hands of the devil can make it. But he is devoted to God and bravely accepts his fate.

It is indeed the case that people who have achieved nothing in life blame everything possible, but do not want to take responsibility for their own "failures.

A successful person is proud of what he has achieved and likes to proclaim, "I did it all by myself.

Unfortunately, such comparisons often focus on material achievements, and successes on a purely human level are not considered as valuable.

And that is what is so important to the drinker. Because of the prevailing status mentality in our society, the addict often has no choice but to compare himself to the people who are considered winners in the eyes of society. No wonder, then, that he sees this prestige as unattainable for him and seeks other ways that will allow him to rise to "hero" status as well. He is then a strong swimmer against the current. At least he thinks he is swimming against the current. When all the world is after filthy lucre, he makes himself an adversary by classifying his professional activities as unimportant from now on.

He, the master of his life and at the same time the plaything of the "dishonest" powers, frees himself from all constraints and masters his life in his own way. Finally, he finds himself in the best of company among his new admirers. In his dazed perceptiveness, "his world in a drunken stupor" appears to him as the only correct answer to all of humanity's problems. He doesn't give a damn about anything. One can only hope that he will come to his senses before it is too late. Once addiction has destroyed the last reserve of a positive outlook on life, there is little hope of salvation.

The descent begins.

THE DEPARTURE

What such a descent looks like depends largely on the net worth of the addict.

There are some very well known personalities who have accumulated considerable wealth through show business that they will not be able to spend for the rest of their lives.

These people have little fear of social or financial decline. They always have enough left over to afford a fancy house and the finest fabrics.

But even here, it is questionable whether they will maintain their social status in the long run.

Admittedly, having a lot of money makes it easier to continue drinking in our materialistic world, but it also limits the personal quality of life. Alcohol makes no difference here. If you think about what a famous drinker could do with his fortune if he were sober instead of hanging out in hotel bars most of the time drunk out of his mind, that's a shame, too.

What will happen to the reputation he has worked so hard for? What's the point of all that stress if alcohol makes you not want to spend your free time recreating and being creative?

Eventually, he will not get any more engagements and will only serve the press as an intermission clown. At least his family will be provided for. If his wife divorces him, she gets a fat settlement and looks for someone else.

But again, this is a very material view. Unfortunately, these spouses often have to deal with even more personal suffering than those in a "normal" marriage.

Actors, pop stars and other members of the entertainment industry are often away from home because of their jobs, which means that their personal lives are neglected.

This is not always easy for the partner. He has to miss out

on a lot of love and closeness, which is very important for a functioning partnership.

Imagine that your loved one, whom you see only twice a month, is drunk every time you meet, and you can feel the pain this causes your sober partner. You can't get enough compensation for that.

I recently read an article about Dean Martin, a great actor. His death was a great loss to Hollywood and to all his fans. He was in the spotlight for many years and enjoyed great popularity. He loved life and all the parties that went with it. The last years he spent drinking in his favorite pub. Only his friend "Alcohol" remained at his side after all the fame of the past years.

I will not presume to judge what caused this man to seek solace in alcohol, only to fall ill and die miserably. What I can imagine, however, is how he would have handled his successes sober and how many roles he could have played in his old age. What a pity.

One thing is clear: the body can take a lot. It is not uncommon for alcoholics to live to a ripe old age without dying prematurely from cirrhosis of the liver.

Anyway, it is a misconception that the liver is the first organ to fall victim to alcohol. Before the liver, the heart, pancreas, stomach, etc., are often affected.

And some heavy drinkers don't get physically sick at all. But what is never, or very rarely, addressed is the psyche. Again and again, upon closer examination, one finds that this part of our being, which makes up our personality, is not taken seriously.

The psyche is the great unknown. And everything we do not know, we reject. In addition, we immediately dismiss illnesses of the psyche as "not being all there. "He goes to a psychiatrist. He's crazy."

If we are suffering from depression or our problems are overwhelming us, we will swallow any pill that promises to alleviate our suffering. Any kind of alcohol will do. We equate going to a psychiatrist or therapist with going to the scaffold. "For heaven's sake. I'm not crazy!"

But the fact that a sick soul destroys our life in the long run is not quite clear to us. And that, for me, is the real descent. We strive for physical perfection, take care to appear healthy, successful, and flawless to the outside world. You know what such a descent can look like in individual cases. No home, no job, no intact social environment - the gutter.

If our psyche is not completely intact, life can very quickly turn into a very long, painful death. Life passes us by. We do everything we can to numb the psyche so that it will just leave us alone.

But the psyche is not so easily numbed. It needs our help to heal. And yet we are ashamed to say, "I have a problem and I'm going to get help to solve it.

We are fully aware that we need help, but we are too ashamed to ask for it. We are sinking slowly but surely. We live with half vitality.

The actual descent is a product of our inner attitude, which we construct through negative thoughts, feelings of shame and false pride, only to make it a reality with the help of alcohol.

That's why everyone who ends up in the gutter is responsible. There are no ifs and buts. Self-pity doesn't help - "I'm a poor, disadvantaged wretch.

As I said at the beginning, no one can help getting addicted, but they are damn responsible for the rest of their lives.

Because addiction is part of our body and mind, it will always be with us, for whatever reason.

Once we have made the decision to live an abstinent life and adjust our lives according to these new requirements, we can change everything for the better. Of course, even with this new philosophy of life, we are not protected from misfortune. But we will always be able to make clear and sober decisions to survive another low.

We must not create a negative future with our thoughts, but constantly imagine how beautiful our life is now and how pleasant our interpersonal relationships have developed and will continue to develop.

This works well only as long as we stop drinking alcohol.

As soon as we start thinking that a little bit of alcohol now and then won't do any harm, and we allow ourselves that little bit of alcohol, we immediately re-evaluate the importance of alcohol and fall back into the old pattern of thinking.

And that pattern of thinking is the basis of the descent. We have to come to terms with the fact that we cannot tolerate alcohol, otherwise the psyche and the body will rebel and our lives will again be negatively affected.

No bum is born a bum. He is the result of a series of wrong values and choices.

Today, no addict has to live like a leper. He gets help everywhere. The only thing he needs is a little insight and the courage to accept that help. With these two components, he will be able to see which paths lead to his descent and which lead to a happy life.

Descent is never pre-programmed.

Rather, it is the result of our habits. The beauty of habits is that we can change them.

If we set high expectations for our lives, we will achieve a lot. When we have a goal in mind, we inevitably develop habits that have a positive impact on our lives, our health, our social standing, and our self-confidence.

So set goals. It doesn't matter if your goals are professional, financial, social, or simply personal. As you plan, make sure that your goals evoke positive feelings in you.

THE PHASE OF THE CONTROLLED USE OF ALCOHOL

The value of alcohol is so high in the addict's mind that all reason and knowledge about the problems of excessive use are usually of little use.

The addict is convinced that his life cannot function without alcohol. He simply cannot imagine socializing without a drink. A life of total abstinence is unthinkable in his eyes.

Since pressure from his family or superiors often increases because of his drinking and puts him in a bind, he works on a double-bottom technique.

He tries to drink in a controlled manner. This type of drinking is a very hard and grueling phase in any alcoholic's career. In fact, it is only one attempt at a time.

Realize one thing: an addict is an addict. There is no compromise.

It is the same with pregnancy. There is no such thing as a little pregnant.

In group discussions, we have regularly found that controlled drinking is a teachable moment for any alcoholic.

Because of the importance of alcohol, this drinking behavior is the highest goal of every drinker. It would make you socially acceptable without attracting attention. Moreover, it would almost be proof that one is not really addicted. After all, one can enjoy the "pleasures" of alcohol without it, or at least to a "normal" degree. Strangely enough, this restriction of alcohol consumption works for quite a while. With willpower, you can actually keep it up for some time.

Personally, I have been able to go days and weeks without drinking. Even when the temptation to drink was strong after a while, I limited myself to a single glass in the presence of my wife. But the urge for "more" was always there.

I desperately wanted to pretend to my wife that I did not have a drinking problem. This burden of proof even drove me to a psychiatrist. Of course, I didn't tell him the whole truth. "I drink two or three bottles of beer now and then," I innocently told him, "so my wife thinks I have a drinking problem." Of course, with this information, he was able to assure me that there was no problem. I then proudly shared the results of this session with my wife.

What she told me years later was that she went to see the psychiatrist shortly thereafter to make sure that his diagnosis was correct. For a while she was actually reassured and not so worried about my condition.

But the carefree time did not last long. My crashes returned at regular intervals and increased in intensity.

Officially, I would have been considered a "quarter drinker" at that time. Strangely enough, this type of alcoholic is considered quite harmless, since the dry periods in between distract from the real suffering, at least for those around them.

The addict himself, however, often suffers even more because he desperately wants to drink again. There are also quarterly drinkers who really rise above themselves during this time and use the temporary dry period for rehabilitation. They exercise, eat healthily, and participate in social life in a normal way without feeling the need to drink alcohol.

As a result, they attract far less unwanted attention than their peers who (must) get drunk every day. They are also under less external pressure to stop drinking.
This circumstance, of course, often prolongs their drinking career. They cheat their way through many years almost unnoticed, without being recognized and exposed as a drunk.
"He likes to have a drink now and then to quench his thirst" is still said almost affectionately.
This state of affairs is tolerable for those around the addict, as long as the addict is not prone to violence during his drinking binges.

In controlled drinking, the addict tries with all his might to distract himself from his craving for alcohol. He wants to appear completely normal and healthy.
This is completely unnatural. Psychological and physical addiction is a disease that destroys not only his own life, but also that of his partner, family, and children.
He will only get out of it if he does something about it. Only he can decide whether he will continue to live in good health or end up as a social case, lonely and abandoned, without any self-respect.

Controlled drinking is a sure sign that an addiction problem is already present. A healthy person does not need to control himself. He has a glass now and then when he feels like it, and he doesn't miss anything if you just put a glass of water in front of him.

PHASES OF DROUGHT

Once the addict realizes that controlled drinking is not working, and external pressure and physical discomfort force him to finally distance himself from alcohol, he makes a decision. Either he continues to drink to the bitter end, until his organs refuse to do their job and cause him a cruel death. But I don't want to go into this option at all. If the addict manages to get sober, that is, to stop drinking abruptly, he first enters a critical phase. Many alcoholics do not realize the danger they are in. They sober up at home on their own, so to speak. I must say this clearly: This is not the right way, because there is a danger to life during alcohol withdrawal. It is imperative that YOU seek medical attention during the acute withdrawal phase!
I would like to explain to you in layman's terms why this is necessary. Over the years, alcohol has taken root in your body. Alcohol is a neurotoxin that has become part of your metabolism through regular use. The body has recognized and accepted it as a "natural" substance. If you now deprive the body of this substance, it sends out warning signals. In the case of deficiency symptoms, such as lack of calcium, magnesium, and iron, the body sends signals so that we can replenish the necessary nutrients and ensure proper functioning.

Failure to recognize these deficiencies can often lead to more serious illnesses.

The situation with alcohol is similar. However, because alcohol is not a substance that the body absolutely needs to survive, the warning signals disappear after a while, although the time cannot be determined.
So the body sends out warning signals that there is an imbalance, triggered by the falling alcohol level. These signals take the form of nervousness, excessive sweating, tremors, and dizziness.
In the worst case, the addict will experience delirium. This sometimes involves severe lapses of consciousness and hallucinations. Chills, convulsions, and failure of vital organs are also common symptoms, often resulting in death.

Withdrawal must therefore be carried out in a hospital under medical supervision. Do not experiment!
Plan your withdrawal well in advance. Talk to your family doctor or go directly to a clinic.
There are counseling centers in every city that can help you and direct you to a place that is suitable for withdrawal.

Take this to heart.

In a hospital, you will be given medications such as distraneurin or doxepin, which will relieve the above symptoms, thus making withdrawal easier and preventing failure symptoms. Be sure to tell your doctor what you have been drinking and how much. Some medications have fatal effects that can cause respiratory failure if taken with alcohol. Don't lie. Honesty starts now!

Do not be afraid. You are not alone. If you need help, contact an addiction counselor who is available at almost any medical facility.

Fortunately, withdrawal patients often stabilize very quickly. Once the acute withdrawal phase is over, the vitality and strength long lost to alcohol abuse return.

The addict feels strong again and fully able to live.

But this phase of addiction is a double-edged sword. When the addict is released from the safe environment of the hospital after withdrawal, he or she is often left alone. This does not mean that help is no longer available, but rather that he believes that he no longer needs help. He is convinced that a miraculous healing has occurred at the same time as the withdrawal. It is a sublime feeling for him not to crave alcohol. In fact, addicts literally blossom during this stage of their drinking career, bursting with confidence. They feel so secure that they don't realize that the addiction is still lurking, and relapse is already waiting in the wings. In this situation, it is extremely important to attend a group in order to recognize the progressions and pitfalls of alcoholism and to react accordingly.

THE RECEPTION

The common belief is that relapse is the moment when the alcoholic reaches for the bottle again, that is, when he ends his sobriety. But this is fundamentally wrong!

Relapse begins much earlier. It first takes place in the addict's mind. When the initial euphoria wears off, in the period shortly after withdrawal, and everyday life resumes its

normal course, many sufferers fall into a depressive hole.
They realize that there are problems even without drinking.
Problems that are actually quite normal and not a major obstacle for any healthy person.

Also, it is understandable that at some point, the praise of relatives for the strong-willed performance of the sick person wears off. There may even be a little criticism, as the now sober partner is expected to show a little more commitment in the household.

After all, for years you could not get any help from him because of his drunkenness.

Then a fight is not far away: "I've stopped drinking and you're still nagging me.

The addict is very, very vulnerable at this stage. His family cannot be expected to know this. Nor does he know that these partial "overreactions" are part of the course of the disease of addiction, and that they occur again and again during the first period of abstinence. Therefore, it is simply a matter of the addict attending a support group immediately after withdrawal to learn what reactions and behaviors can occur. This is the only way he will understand how to correctly assess his behavior in the future and be able to take appropriate measures in time to prevent the escalation of feelings.

It is also helpful to discuss what you have learned with your partner. It is best to attend the group together. After all, partners now face problems in dealing with the addict that they cannot solve alone.

If a group visit or therapy in a specialized clinic does not take place, alcohol-specific difficulties are added to the usual everyday and relationship problems, and relapse is pre-programmed.

There is simply no experience of how addiction manifests itself during periods of dryness. Entrenched patterns of behavior are deeply ingrained.

 Even if the previously dry alcoholic has not yet reached for the bottle, he may already be thinking about what it would be like to "just" have a beer. One must never forget the importance that alcohol had during the wet period. Addiction does not give up this status easily.

It fights with all its might to regain the upper hand.

"Just one beer. After that, I'll stop right away". This single thought is the real relapse. This is where he makes his decision. He simply cannot imagine a life without alcohol.

From then on, it is only a matter of time before he acts on this thought.

As soon as he opens the bottle and drinks that "one" beer, a familiar cycle is set in motion. Because of the perhaps longer abstinence period, he firmly believes that he has overcome the original addiction. Either he lets himself get drunk, confident that he will be sober the next morning, or he drinks just that one beer - in other words, he drinks again in a controlled way.

To be clear, both are clearly addictive drinking. Even if at first glance it seems that he would have no trouble quitting after one beer. Anything is possible. And as soon as he realizes that it is possible to stop drinking after one bottle, he may already be mentally preparing for the next attempt.

"What can happen? Last time I had enough after one bottle," he tells himself. Maybe he will stay with one bottle many times. But the time comes when one bottle becomes two and two becomes three. It usually doesn't take long for the person to fall back into the same rut.

Only then is the relapse recognized as such. By then it may be too late. The consequences are well known from what we have read so far.

To prevent relapse, I advise you to take thoughts of drinking very seriously. As soon as you notice that you sometimes feel like reaching for the bottle, talk to someone about it. Either in a group or with your partner. Even if you have an open, trusting relationship with your partner, keep in mind that you may be frightening him or her with your thoughts about alcohol.

After all, he or she will care about you, and your wet past may be worse in his or her mind than yours.

Give yourself a break and really go to an anonymous group where you can get expert help and advice to overcome your problems and fears.

If you are serious about dealing with your alcohol problem, there is no way around it.

THE AWAKENING

Setbacks are often severe. Disappointment at the lack of stamina and the scolding of family and friends add to the already battered self-confidence.

It is not uncommon for a relapse to result in an increase in alcohol tolerance, which means that the person often drinks even more than in the previous drinking phase. Of course, this is not only physically harmful. Psychological dependence also increases.

In order to remain reasonably fit for life and society, he must maintain a certain level of alcohol. Due to increasing alcohol tolerance, it becomes difficult to consume alcohol in the form of "light" drinks, as this simply requires too much liquid. It also takes too long to reach the required level.

That's why many people switch to high-proof drinks during this phase. Vodka, cognac, whiskey and other drinks now become the companion and drive the addict faster and faster to ruin.

Once he is in this state of constant drunkenness, not only does his inner struggle with addiction intensify, but so does that of his social environment.

He can no longer perform his job. Everything becomes too much. His boss may threaten to fire him, his wife may threaten to divorce him.

Usually the pressure becomes so great that he wakes up from his dilemma between drunkenness and frustration.

It is well known among dry alcoholics that everyone has to reach their own particular low point in order to make a lasting change in their lives. For many, this low point is the loss of a job or divorce. Others, however, are so physically and emotionally at the end of their rope that there is simply no other way than the road to sobriety.

After another period of withdrawal, he realizes that there is no turning back. Of course, there are many addicts who have to go through this process of withdrawal and relapse many times before they finally realize that alcohol is ruining their lives.

THE SEARCH FOR HELP

Because of all the resistance he has built up through his drinking, he will initially be on his own. After all, he has shamelessly exploited and tested the trust of his family, friends, and superiors, and now he must do everything in his power to regain it.

The most important thing is his trust in himself. He is also disappointed in himself. It is not uncommon for strong feelings of guilt to weigh on his soul. He needs to learn that what happened cannot be undone. He will not necessarily be able to count on the best treatment from his relatives in the initial period. He will need help to process all this. He is probably responsible for his actions, but the disease as such also plays a significant role.

Addiction wants to be satisfied. It drives people to use substances in varying amounts to satisfy their cravings. Ultimately, man lives only to satisfy his insatiable desire. In the process, his nature changes so much that he becomes a truly different person.

His personal qualities and goals take a back seat to his addiction. He is no longer himself.

This is typical of addictions in general and alcohol addiction in particular. He needs to understand this so he doesn't let guilt block his path to a sober, satisfied future.

If he is willing to seek help on his own, he has a good chance of overcoming the addiction and its negative impact on his life. Attending a support group may be the first time he feels he is not alone with his thoughts, feelings, and worries.

It is precisely because of the pent-up feelings of guilt that he needs to vent. This does not mean that he is forgiven for everything, but he learns that he is only partly to blame, and that he must take responsibility for his future actions. He can't help being addicted, but he has the power to stop the disease.

The importance of alcohol must be replaced by other life-affirming things. He will learn to analyze and overcome problems soberly. Problems are special landmarks in life that are often triggers for better performance. One could also say that the more problems a person solves over time, the more his self-confidence and self-esteem grow, because he has taken responsibility for them.

It is often observed that others are always blamed for failures in life. When something goes well, when a mission is crowned with success, one's chest swells and one proudly declares that one did it all by oneself.

A (wet) alcoholic, if we look at him from the point of view of self-esteem, really cannot grow in life. After all, he is not able to cope with problems all by himself.

For the smallest obstacles, he needs a ladder in the form of liquor, beer, or wine. How can pride and respect develop there? In his eyes, he must inevitably see himself as a wimp. But he would be only too happy to collect the laurels himself.

That is why many people drink secretly to hide the liquid helper. They think no one will notice. But the signs of addictive drinking cannot be hidden, at least not in the long run.

THE ABSOLUTE SURRENDER

As soon as the drinker realizes that he is only hurting himself by hiding, he is ready to accept the disease and give up. He surrenders. He now knows that he cannot fight the addiction.

He no longer gives alcohol power over his life. He will do everything he can to live a sober life. In the surrender phase, he accepts help, of which there is plenty. He joins a group or goes to rehab.
Now he has a good chance of breaking the vicious cycle of drinking-withdrawal-relapse. He is open to constructive criticism and advice.
He realizes there is no other way out.

Surrender is followed by further withdrawal. Either as an inpatient in a hospital or in a special facility for addicts.
The addiction has now brought him to his personal low point. He doesn't want to sink any deeper.
This very word - will - is crucial to the success of his intentions.
With "I don't want it anymore" he takes responsibility. Even though it may be "I can't anymore" in the beginning. But that doesn't matter right now. In any case, he is ready to do something. It also doesn't matter if he made the decision on his own, without any pressure from outside, or if he was prompted to do so.

The important thing is that he admits his illness. Only the goal is important.

THE THERAPY

There are several ways to get clean. Inpatient therapy, outpatient therapy, or regular group meetings.

The addict alone decides which way to go. In my experience, gained from many conversations with dry alcoholics, residential therapy is probably the safest way out of addiction.

On the one hand, he can go through acute withdrawal directly in a health resort (although some facilities require the "patient" to start his stay sober). How this is regulated in detail, you must clarify with the counseling center located in your place). In addition, he or she will be given medication to prevent worsening withdrawal symptoms. Second, after withdrawal, he is immediately under expert supervision and away from any danger zones.

During his stay at the spa, he receives important support on the subject of alcoholism in individual and group therapy. Here he learns how to live his life "without" alcohol.

He also has the opportunity to solve problems that are not directly related to alcohol.

In addition, inpatient therapy gives him the time and peace to focus on himself, away from his job, family and friends. He is the center of attention. That is very important.

The advantage of an inpatient stay is clearly the concentrated absorption of information and the wide range of therapies. In a relatively short time *(the duration depends on the individual condition of each patient),* the addict learns everything about alcohol addiction and its treatment options.

Even after this renewed measure, further group visits are still appropriate. Because, as already described, a cure of several weeks is again not enough. The disease, even if it has been stopped, requires full attention.

THE DIFFERENCE BETWEEN STAYING DRY AND BEING DRY.

Once someone stops drinking alcohol, we usually consider them "dry. For the addict, however, there is a huge difference that is crucial to lasting sobriety.

It may seem like a pun at first, but I want to make it clear to you what is at stake and why this little hair-splitting is so important.

Staying dry" is purely a matter of will once withdrawal has taken place. At this stage, it is perfectly normal for thoughts of varying intensity to arise from time to time, reminding the addict of how good the beer tasted and how good it felt to drink it. After a long time, we humans only remember the good things. This is true of everything in life.

When grown men today remember their time in the Bundeswehr, they only think of the funny and especially outrageous things that happened during their service.

Nobody thinks about the terrible food and the sometimes nonsensical services. Even when it comes to vacation memories, we quickly forget the unpleasant things, while we still remember the beautiful sunset on the beach years later.

So why shouldn't an alcoholic feel the same way? He has memories, too. Especially of the time when alcohol was not yet a problem. Especially during the addictive drinking phase, things happened that he remembers fondly.

And that's the rub. He must learn to process his memories properly. But the alcohol should not be the focus. The beautiful things, which might have been even more beautiful without alcohol, should take first place.

And this is where an unwavering will helps. It makes it possible to direct thoughts about alcohol into realistic channels.

Because of our fond memories, we find it increasingly difficult to keep the bad sides of alcohol in mind. And we should.

In the group, we tell our personal stories over and over again. It is usually quite detailed. We consciously remember the impossible things we did when we were drunk. Things that were sometimes life-threatening. Life-threatening not only to ourselves, but to others as well. This is the only way we stay on the ball. We are close to our problem.

I have talked to many people who had more alcohol than blood in their veins during their drinking years and still got behind the wheel of their car.

Imagine what YOUR life would be like if you had run over a child while drunk. These thoughts are horrible, but very useful in your current situation.

However, it is part of the recovery process that at first people still like to think about the joyful moments. This is why it is important to keep yourself sober at will.

WITHOUT A STRONG WILL, IT WON'T WORK - BUT THE WILL ALONE IS NOT ENOUGH!

There are also dry alcoholics who have been abstinent for years. They know that they are "not allowed" to drink again, lest they fall back into the vicious cycle.

It takes a tremendous amount of strength and perseverance. In a way, I admire these people, but in no way do I envy them, because they are secretly grieving. Actually, they would like to take another punch in the chest. But their common sense forbids it.

Reason is all well and good, but I prefer passion and joie de

ॐ

vivre.

Only when you can enjoy not drinking can you talk about being sober. Anything else is a stubborn attitude and a time bomb. A time bomb, because the moment will come when the person concerned is overloaded. In the time when everything is going normally and he only has to pay attention to fighting his alcohol problem, he might make it.
But when something unexpected happens, the death of a loved one or some other dramatic event, in many cases there is an overload.
As a result, he can easily fall back into old patterns. That's why I always focus my attention on the positive processing of my addiction. Not that I repress anything, but I replace negative feelings and behaviors with positive ones, always consulting my bad memories of my wet time.
When I went through inpatient withdrawal, the doctor in charge told me, "If you want to live to be 40, you must never drink another drop!"
Can you imagine the effect of those words on a 30 year old? I turned white and trembled for my life.
Unfortunately, I didn't have much support during my first withdrawal. I was not informed about treatment options, nor was I given an address to go to.
But the doctor's testimony later ensured that I got better. My main problem was two words - "not allowed". I had always hated bans. But now these words affected everything I was attached to.
At the time, I could not imagine ever drinking again. But in my group, I soon realized how to take positive things out of the doctor's statement.
I learned to turn "I can't" into "I WON'T." All it takes is absolute honesty about alcohol. I wanted to live, and I

wanted to learn everything I could about my disease. So I listened to the advice of the group members.

As soon as one of my old acquaintances asked me if I wanted to join in the drinking, I proudly replied, "No, thank you. I don't want to drink alcohol. I prefer a glass of mineral water. In the beginning, I was dying for someone to ask me what I wanted to drink. For years the answer had been clear. Now I was able to break a habit that had become an addiction and replace it with a healthy, life-affirming one.

And the more I said, "I don't want it," the better I felt.

THE SATISFACTION

What is needed on the road to sobriety and satisfaction is a clear commitment.

Namely, you have to own your addiction from the beginning. "Yes, I'm an alcoholic. A dry alcoholic!" You don't have to beat this fact into everyone's head, but rather use it as a strategy that will ultimately benefit you in the long run.

As soon as you become an active participant in a group and stop drinking alcohol, it happens that they are offered far more alcoholic beverages than before. You are now in a bind. And since there are two sides to everything in life, take the opportunity to grow from it.

Own your disease by taking a positive offensive. "No, thank you. An apple spritzer tastes better to me." You will strengthen your will even more if you close all doors behind you.

This means that you should first tell your family and friends about your illness. Tell them openly and honestly that you have your alcohol problem and that you don't want to drink in the future. This will kill several birds with one stone. First, they will not be offered alcohol in the future, and second, you will avoid people whispering behind your back, because everyone who knows you has already noticed that you have changed: "You already saw. X doesn't drink anymore". By publicly admitting your problem, you will gain a reputation.

You will see how positively people respond to your new attitude. Your clear statement of intent will also make it harder for you to relapse during a period of weakness. It will be harder to get alcohol anywhere because everyone knows the consequences. You will build a kind of protective wall around yourself, which will also awaken your conscience as soon as the thought of alcohol creeps in.

Your clear confession gives you self-confidence and self-esteem. It gives you the opportunity to assert yourself sober and without outside help. You will enjoy showing how strong and safe you are in society without alcohol.

Besides the people who have never drunk alcohol in their lives, you will find that there are many people who have experienced the same thing as you.

Think of yourself and your health. You are now the center of attention. Before you worry about broken friendships that have fallen victim to your addiction, think about yourself first. Everything else can wait. Also, it will not work to correct all the mistakes you made during your wet time.

Don't dwell on your guilt. The fact that you made mistakes and hurt others is not very nice, but you were not the only one responsible. Alcoholism is a multifaceted disease. The addict does things that are not in his nature. He lives only for the addiction. Therefore, he is only partly responsible for what he does during the drinking phase.

If you are in recovery and the feelings of guilt become too strong, discuss them with your support group. You are sure to get suggestions that will help you in this acute situation.

I also had to make amends at that time. However, knowing that the people I had offended in my drunken stupor would probably be difficult to appease, and that a friendship like the one that originally existed would probably not blossom again, I thought a bit selfishly. For the time being, I just wanted to clear my conscience so that I could recover in peace. So I wrote a letter to the people I still cared about, telling them about my drinking problem and that I was now sober. If they wanted to give me another chance, I would be happy to hear from them.

By the way, only one of the nine people I wrote to got back to me. But that did not matter. I had gotten what was bothering me off my chest and was relieved.

Focus your attention solely on your inner contentment. Any means will do. It is all about YOU.

THE PHOENIX FROM THE ASHES

With dryness, you get a second chance to rebuild your life. How many people are lucky enough to start over?

So your disease has its advantages. How quickly you get back on your feet depends on them. But don't rush into anything. Only when you feel the joy of a life without alcohol from deep within will you be ready to focus on your goals in the long term.

Because of your maturity and life experience, your second chance is a unique event. You are now able to consciously "experience" your life. They can enjoy everything much better because they always have a comparison before their eyes.

Dry alcoholics are often capable of tremendous accomplishments. They also have an immense need to actively participate in life. Like a phoenix from the ashes, they suddenly rise from obscurity.

They become valued members of the family, and their newfound self-confidence and self-esteem enable them to open up to others. Professionally, everything is open to them again.

However, caution is advised. Self-confidence, self-esteem, and renewed energy can also lead to overestimating yourself. Don't expect too much from yourself. Even if you want to satisfy your need to catch up, you should always keep in mind that you are not cured forever. As I said, the disease cannot be cured, it can only be stopped.

Therefore, it is very important that you pay attention to the warning signals of your body. Despite their dryness and self-confidence, they are not girls for everything. Often, dry alcoholics lurch from one addiction to another. They used to be alcoholics, now they are workaholics. Those who take on too much easily become stressed, and stress causes physical and mental exhaustion. And as soon as we are no longer mentally free and our bodies are tired and exhausted, the dormant addiction sees another opportunity to reclaim land.

Don't give addiction a chance. Know your limits and set them clearly. Say "NO" once in a while. You have no obligation to anyone.

It is quite clear that at first the guilty conscience triumphs over reason and we offer any help we can to make amends. But this is the wrong way. The most important thing is a lasting, satisfying sobriety.

When you finally reach for the bottle out of sheer exhaustion, all the fingers will point at you. It is not the others who will feel guilty because they used their services unconditionally. YOU will be the guilty one again.

"He/she is just a hopeless case," they will say.

THE INCONVENIENT MAN

Precisely because getting and staying sober involves putting your personal needs first, you often come across as selfish. But healthy selfishness is extraordinarily important for a healthy life. During the drinking phase, it is very common to see a person who, in order to distract himself from his addiction, never says "no," even when he wants to. Especially during the first period of dryness, he is too often willing to do whatever is asked of him because of his guilty conscience.

It is only in the course of recovery that he begins to recognize his own desires and needs, as well as his limits, and because of the self-confidence he has gained, he is able to say "no" from time to time. These are, of course, completely new sounds to those around him.

Suddenly, he has matured into a new personality who makes independent decisions about his life. No wonder there is friction.

So as not to provoke unnecessary arguments with your family and friends, explain to them in advance that you are no longer willing to do everything with blind obedience. Tell them that this is of utmost importance for their future lives and ask them to understand.

The more open you are about the ways out of addiction, the more support you can expect. If you're alone in your new life, you can't expect everyone to understand. Be open with your loved ones. By sharing your intentions with them, you will gain their trust and support.

Your loved ones do not want to see you change your mind again.

In their group discussions, you will learn many more suggestions that will help them to keep their social environment relaxed. It is important that you feel comfortable. Free from psychological tensions, even though it is inevitable in the personal sphere that there will be discussions from time to time. Where people live together, there will be disagreements and debates. But if your actions can counteract problems as they arise, there's nothing wrong with that, right?

Final words

In this book, I have described many motivations and obstacles that cross the path leading out of alcoholism. In my group discussions, however, many more problems and help have come up. It would be inconceivable to put them all in writing. It would go beyond any scope.

That is why I always urge you to "go to a support group as soon as possible.

It makes everything easier. That's not to say I don't think you have the grit, but this problem is too complex to work through alone in a quiet room. It could take you a hundred years. And of course you don't have that kind of time.

You don't have to reinvent the wheel. Fortunately, a lot of people thought about how to break addiction before you did. Since you have now read several times that it is only up to you whether you make it or not, I suggest that you stop wasting time.

I wish you contented sobriety, good health and joy of life.

"All things for which you ask, believe that you receive them, and they shall be given you". Mark 11:24

End

ॐ

ॐ